Madhur Jaffrey's Cookbook

This book is dedicated
with
much love and gratitude
to
Aleene and Willis Allen
(the best parents-in-law I know)
whom I have pestered
with questions
(culinary and otherwise)
these last twenty years

First published in Great Britain in 1987 by
Pavilion Books Limited,
196 Shaftesbury Avenue, London WC2H 8JL
in association with Michael Joseph Limited,
27 Wrights Lane, Kensington, London W8 5TZ

Text © Madhur Jaffrey 1987
Colour illustrations © 1987 Farida Zaman
Black and white illustrations © 1987 Jo Laurence
Photographs by James Jackson

British Library Cataloguing in Publication Data
Jaffrey, Madhur
    Madhur Jaffrey's cookbook: food for
family and friends.
    1. Cookery, International
    I. Title
    641.5   TX725.A1

        ISBN   1-85145-152-8

Printed and bound in Italy by Arnoldo Mondadori

*Measurements in this book are given in imperial
quantities with metric and American
equivalents. When measuring ingredients,
follow one system throughout.*

MADHUR JAFFREY'S COOKBOOK

FOOD FOR FAMILY AND FRIENDS

PAVILION
MICHAEL JOSEPH

CONTENTS

INTRODUCTION

I am stretched out on an easy chair under my favourite maple tree, reading, dreaming a little, when a thought comes flitting by. It would be very pleasant to see some dear friends who live a few hills away. I rise, confer – barefooted – with my husband who is lost in his admiration of this year's crop of lilies, then go indoors to telephone our friends. They are free and will come. We are all delighted.

It is already afternoon. What am I going to cook? I do not want the sense of summer ease to end. I do not want to drive myself to distraction. Yet, I do want the evening to be imbued with a certain degree of elegance and grace. I want the food to be superb – how could I be satisfied with anything else? – and the cooking to be easy. It *can* be done.

Here, in this book, are dozens of such meals – meals that I cook all the time for my family and friends. Some consist of nothing more than a warming soup. There is a Thai noodle soup here with bits of vegetables floating in it that you season yourself at the table with an array of condiments – crushed peanuts, green coriander (Chinese parsley) and home-made sauces. It almost forces friendliness and chatter as all hands reach across the table to get a little more of this or that. For bone-chilling, blustery days, there is a hearty meal of succulent, soy-flavoured pork chops that I serve with a mixture of mashed yellow turnips and potatoes (they call it 'neeps and taters' in Scotland) and a quickly made fennel-flavoured dish of stir-fried cabbage.

If there is a greater emphasis on light dishes – steamed fish dressed with soy sauce and roasted sesame seeds, grilled chicken kebabs on a bed of stir-fried watercress – it is only because that is how we eat. We are careful about how much dark meat, eggs, butter and cream we consume. But certainly not to the point of fanaticism. If we feel like grilling a butterflied leg of lamb one day, encrusted with crushed red and black pepper, we do. The next day, we have some simply grilled salmon served with a mustard-flecked yoghurt and fresh tomato sauce.

The foods in this book are not just from India, where I was born, or from America, the land I have happily adopted. They are from wherever I have been in the past fifty years, wherever I have eaten. They are the sum of my experience, blending cooking techniques and seasonings from all over the world.

I travel a lot and could be said to have eaten my way through the continents many times over. Today, when I go to the market and see, say, a pile of crisp, fresh green beans, dozens of possibilities start to buzz in my head. Should I cook then Szechuan-style with garlic, red pepper and soy sauce or stir-fry them with a mound of shallots and strips of pork the way I had them on a beach in Bali? Of course, I could blanch them and douse them with a mustardy French vinaigrette, or, on the other hand, I could stir-fry them with cumin and ginger as we do in India. Sometimes I follow the specific regional style of a particular country and at other times I blend styles, making, say, a vinaigrette sauce with the addition of cumin and ginger. (And very good it is too.)

Being Indian, I'm naturally familiar with a vast spectrum of spices and know all the simple tricks and techniques that can draw out many almost contradictory flavours from the same spice. Mustard seeds, for example, can be very hot and pungent when crushed. They turn amazingly sweet and nutty if they are thrown into a little hot oil and allowed to pop. The popping seems to dissipate their anger. If you are cooking some greens, you probably know how good they would be if you were to sauté them with oil and garlic. If, however, you were to sauté them with garlic *and* popped mustard seeds, they would be heavenly.

The spices and seasonings I have used throughout this book are easy to find in supermarkets and health food stores. I want the cooking to be easy. I do not want the shopping to be an impossible pain. Most spices here will be familiar to you. The way they are used may not. If I am browning chicken, for example, and want a flavour of cinnamon, I throw a whole cinnamon stick into the hot oil *before* I put in the meat. This way, the hot oil performs two functions: it sears the meat and it also sends an intensified cinnamon flavour shooting through it with the speed of an injection.

I have decided to break the book up into menus so you know at a glance just what vegetables to cook with what meat. Of course, you can move dishes around at will, if that is what you wish. There is a menu for soft summer days featuring a cooling, lemon-flavoured, minty shrimp soup, brimming over with a julienne of fresh vegetables. A picnic menu has a scrumptious hot and sour Thai chicken salad wrapped up in lettuce leaves. There are brunch menus, menus for elegant feasts, and even menus for guests you want to bring home with you after a night at the theatre or opera.

The menus have been grouped into chapters according to whether the main dish is based on fish, chicken or meat, or whether the meal consists primarily of a soup. Next comes a chapter on brunches and teas, and finally one on dessert recipes. On the whole, we tend to eat fruit after our meals, but sometimes I make simple fruit desserts or serve a cake or cookies with our coffee. I have collected a few such recipes and put them at the back of the book. You may pick any you like and add it to any of these menus.

Even as I write, pears are poaching in the kitchen and chicken is marinating. I'm expecting friends tonight. I'm not worried!

FISH FOREMOST

LIGHT AND VERY ELEGANT

ASPARAGUS WITH PRAWNS (SHRIMP)
STEAMED WHOLE FISH WITH SESAME SEED DRESSING
RICE WITH MUSHROOMS, GREEN PEPPER AND BEANS

There are many of our friends – and our daughters' friends – who do not eat red meat. Here is one of the dinners I frequently make for them. I set the fish to steam just before we sit down to eat. Then I serve the first course, which is already prepared, either at room temperature or cold (but with the intense chill of the refrigerator taken off it). By the time we finish the asparagus and prawns (shrimp), the fish is usually ready. As for the rice, I have all the vegetables for it chopped well ahead of time. I invariably set the rice to cook about 10 minutes before the guests arrive. I set a timer so, wherever I am, I can hear when it is done and can turn off the heat. If left covered in a warm place, the rice stays hot for a good 45 minutes or more.

This is a very easy meal to organize – and very delicious to boot.

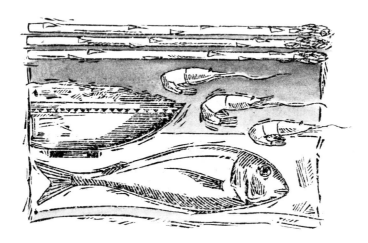

ASPARAGUS WITH PRAWNS (SHRIMP)

Serves 4

This dish was born strangely. One day I had cooked asparagus in a Chinese style for lunch and my husband had sautéed prawns (shrimp) in an Italian style for dinner. The first dish had been flavoured with sesame oil and the second dish with olive oil. There were leftovers at both meals and I had carefuly packed them in separate plastic containers and refrigerated them. Next day, a friend dropped in unexpectedly for dinner. We decided to make pasta for the main course – we had all the ingredients – but what would we do for a starter? It was sorely needed. I opened the refrigerator and stared at it for a moment. Then I emptied the two containers of asparagus and prawns (shrimp) into a single bowl and threw a salad dressing over them. Voilà! A new amazingly good dish was born. Here it is:

For the Asparagus

1¾lb/800g asparagus, of medium thickness
1 tablespoon/15ml peanut oil
About ½ teaspoon/2.5ml salt, or less
1 tablespoon/15ml oriental sesame oil

For the Prawns (Shrimp)

4 tablespoons/60ml olive oil
1–2 cloves garlic, peeled and finely chopped
1 lb/450g medium-sized prawns (shrimp), peeled and deveined
¼ teaspoon salt
1 tablespoon/15ml finely chopped fresh parsley

The Dressing for Both

1 tablespoon/15ml red wine vinegar
1 tablespoon/15ml Dijon-style mustard
Freshly ground black pepper
Salt, if needed

Trim away the woody section of the asparagus spears and peel the lower half. Cut into 2-in/5-cm lengths. Heat the vegetable oil in a frying pan over a medium-high flame. When hot, put in the asparagus, stir and fry for half a minute or until the asparagus turns bright green. Add salt and stir. Add 4 tablespoons/60ml water and bring to a boil. Cover, turn heat to medium-low and simmer for 2–4 minutes or until the asparagus is crisp-tender. Remove the lid, add the sesame oil and turn the heat up a bit to boil all the liquid away. Put the asparagus in a bowl. Cover and refrigerate if required.

Heat the olive oil in a frying pan over a medium-high flame. When very hot, put in the garlic. Stir once and put in the prawns (shrimp) and salt. Stir and fry for 2–4 minutes until just cooked through. Remove the prawns (shrimp) with a slotted spoon and put in a bowl. Throw the parsley into the hot oil. Stir once or twice and empty the oil with the parsley over the prawns (shrimp). Cover and refrigerate if necessary.

Put the vinegar, mustard, black pepper and a pinch of salt in a small bowl. Mix. Pour the oil out of the prawn (shrimp) container, a tablespoon/15ml at a time and beat it into the dressing.

Combine the prawns (shrimp) and asparagus. Pour the dressing over the top and toss. Taste for salt. Serve at room temperature or cold.

Overleaf
CLOCKWISE FROM THE TOP: RICE WITH MUSH-ROOMS, GREEN PEPPER AND BEANS, ASPARAGUS WITH PRAWNS (SHRIMP), STEAMED WHOLE FISH WITH SESAME SEED DRESSING

STEAMED WHOLE FISH WITH SESAME SEED DRESSING

Serves 4

This is a delicate and scrumptious dish of Korean ancestry, quite inspired in its blend of salty, sweet, sour and nutty flavours. Its preparation is quite easy. All that you require is a very fresh fish.

I usually use red snapper, but black bass, striped and sea bass, flounder and even brook trout may be substituted. You will have to find a utensil large enough to steam the fish. I use a 14-in/35-cm wok, inside which I lay 4 wooden chopsticks, each pair at right angles to the other. I set an oval dish (the sort of plate that holds cooked roasts) over the chopsticks. I can fit a 2lb/900g fish in just by trimming the tail slightly. The boiling water is always kept at least 1in/2.5cm below the bottom of the oval dish. My wok does have a domed lid, so that completes the list of my fish steaming equipment.

If you do not have a wok, use a very wide pot. Set a water-filled bowl or trivet on the bottom and balance your fish dish on top of that. Again, make sure that the boiling water stays 1in/2.5cm below the plate. Domed wok lids have an advantage in steaming: the condensing vapour rolls off to the sides and does not fall on the uncovered food. If your lid is flat, line its underside with a dish towel, flopping its ends over the top of the lid so they do not burn.

A whole, fresh, 2lb/900g fish, gutted, scaled and cleaned but with head and tail left on
Salt
Freshly ground black pepper
1 spring onion (scallion)
4 thin slices of peeled fresh ginger, cut crosswise off the root
4 medium-sized mushrooms, sliced
4 thin slices lemon, cut crosswise

Wash the fish and pat dry. Cut deep, diagonal gashes on either side, about 1½in/4cm apart. Sprinkle lightly, inside and out, with salt and black pepper.

Cut the spring onion (scallion) into 1½-in/4-cm lengths. Cut each segment, lengthwise, into fine strips. Stack the ginger slices together and cut into fine strips.

Lay the fish in the steaming dish. Put some spring onion (scallion) and ginger slices under it, some inside it and scatter some over the top. Scatter mushrooms around it. Lay the lemon slices over the length of the fish.

Arrange your utensil for steaming as suggested above and bring the water in it to a rolling boil. Set the dish with the fish over the chopsticks (or trivet). Cover and steam for about 20 minutes or until the fish is just done. Keep a kettle of boiling water ready just in case you need to replenish what is in the wok.

For the Dressing

4fl oz/120ml/½ cup soy sauce
1 clove garlic, peeled and crushed to a pulp
1 tablespoon/15ml oriental sesame oil
2 teaspoons/10ml sugar
½ teaspoon/2.5ml cayenne pepper
2 teaspoons/10ml distilled white vinegar
3 spring onions (scallions), cut into fine rings all the way up their green sections
2 tablespoons/30ml sesame seeds

While the fish is steaming, make the dressing. Combine the soy sauce, garlic, sesame oil, sugar, cayenne pepper, vinegar and spring onions (scallions) in a bowl. Stir to mix. Heat a small cast-iron frying pan over a medium-high flame. When hot, put in the sesame seeds. Stir and roast for 2–3 minutes or until the seeds begin to pop and smell roasted. Add to the bowl with the dressing.

When the fish is done, remove the dish from the wok. (There will be some liquid in it but that is as it should be.) Pour the dressing over the fish and serve immediately.

RICE WITH MUSHROOMS, GREEN PEPPER AND BEANS

Serves 4

This amount of rice may seem a bit excessive for four people – but it *is* a delicious casserole of sorts and helps to soak up all the good fish juices from the preceding recipe.

Long grain rice measured to the 15-fl oz/425-ml/2 cup level in a glass measuring jug
2 tablespoons/30ml peanut or other vegetable oil
1 small onion, peeled and sliced into fine half-rings
1 clove garlic, peeled and finely chopped
8 medium-sized mushrooms, sliced
8 green beans, trimmed and cut into 1-in/2.5-cm lengths
Half a sweet green pepper, cut into ¼-in/6-mm wide lengths and then into 1-in/2.5-cm strips
1 pint/570ml/2½ cups chicken broth or beef broth or any poultry or meat stock (home-made or canned)
Salt to taste (adjusted to the salt in the broth)

Wash the rice in several changes of water. Drain. Put in a bowl and leave to soak for 30 minutes. Drain thoroughly.

Heat the oil in a medium-sized heavy pot over a medium-high flame. When hot, put in the onion and garlic. Stir and fry until the onion browns at the edges. Put in the mushrooms, stir for a minute. Add the green beans and green pepper. Stir another 2 minutes. Put in the drained rice. Stir gently, turning the heat down a bit if the rice starts to stick, for 2 minutes, until the rice turns translucent. Add the broth and salt to taste. (If you dip your finger into the pot and then lick it, it should taste just a wee bit saltier than your palate likes.) Bring to a boil, cover, turn heat to very low, and cook for 25 minutes.

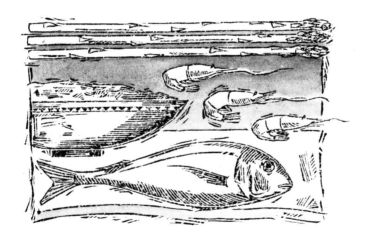

TEMPTATIONS FROM ANGLO-INDIA

FISH FILLETS ON A BED OF SPINACH WITH A
FENNEL-TOMATO SAUCE
GINGERY CAULIFLOWER WITH GRATED CHEESE
BOILED NEW POTATOES WITH ROSEMARY AND PARSLEY

There are times when one wants a light – but not bland – fish dinner. Here the thick fillets of grilled (broiled) fish are served on a bed of spinach, all nicely doused with a fennel-flavoured sauce of tomatoes and onions. On the side is a mild but quite gingery dish of stir-fried cauliflower, invented by my grandmother who decided one day to toss some grated cheese into a very Indian dish. It is uncommonly good. So are the potatoes, with their gentle hint of rosemary.

I generally make the tomato sauce well ahead of time. The potatoes, too, can be made an hour or so in advance and left in a warming oven. The parsley, however, should be sprinkled on at the last minute. The spinach can be cooked in advance and dressed. You can reheat it quickly in its dressing over a low flame. The only two things I like to do just before dinner are the grilling (broiling) of the fish and the stir-frying of the cauliflower. If you have everything cut and ready for the cauliflower, the actual stir-frying can be done while the fish is being cooked.

FISH FILLETS ON A BED OF SPINACH WITH A FENNEL-TOMATO SAUCE

Serves 4

Even though this dish has three parts to it, it is simple to put together and can be made within an hour. The tomato sauce can be made up to two days ahead of time and refrigerated. The biggest chore is washing and trimming fresh spinach. Luckily for us, many supermarkets sell 10-oz/285-g packages of the vegetable already cleaned for our convenience. If you can get them, use them by all means.

I steam my spinach (see below), but you can easily blanch the spinach by dropping it into a large pot of boiling water for a few minutes until it is just wilted and then draining it.

I have used fish fillets here, but fish steaks could easily be substituted. The grilling (broiling) time for the fish will, of course, vary with its thickness. It should brown lightly on the top and just cook through.

For the Tomato Sauce

3 tablespoons/45ml olive oil
2 teaspoons/10ml whole yellow mustard seeds
½ teaspoon/2.5ml whole fennel seeds
1 medium-sized onion, peeled and chopped
2 cloves garlic, peeled and chopped
A 28-oz/800-g can whole tomatoes
¼ teaspoon crushed hot red pepper flakes or ⅛ teaspoon cayenne pepper (optional)
Freshly ground black pepper
Salt

For the Fish

1½lb/675g skinned, thick-cut fillets of haddock, halibut, cod or scrod
2 tablespoons/30ml olive oil or other vegetable oil
1 tablespoon/15ml butter, cut into small pieces
Salt
Freshly ground black pepper

For the Spinach

About 1¼lb/560g spinach, trimmed and washed
4 tablespoons/60ml olive oil
4 teaspoons/20ml red wine vinegar
½ teaspoon/2.5ml salt
Freshly ground black pepper

The tomato sauce

Heat the oil in a frying pan, over a medium-high flame. When hot, put in the mustard seeds and fennel seeds. As soon as the mustard seeds begin to pop (this takes just a few seconds), put in the onion. Stir and fry until the onion turns brown at the edges. Put in the garlic and stir once or twice. Now put in the tomatoes, the liquid in the can, and the crushed red pepper. Cook on a medium-low flame for about 20 minutes, or until the sauce is no longer watery. Add salt to taste and grind in some black pepper. Mix. Keep warm if eating soon.

The spinach

Arrange your steaming equipment. I set a large colander over a large pot that has just enough boiling water in it to stay about ½in/1.5cm below the colander. Put the spinach in the colander. Cover and steam for a few minutes until the spinach has wilted and is just done. Lift the colander with the spinach and squeeze out as much liquid as possible by pressing down with a slotted spoon. Put the spinach in a bowl and dress with oil, vinegar, salt and pepper. Keep warm.

The fish

Preheat the grill (broiler).

Rub the fish with oil and lay it in a single layer on a foil-lined baking tray. Scatter butter pieces on top. Sprinkle lightly with salt and pepper. If the fish is more than ½in/1.5cm thick, pour about 4 tablespoons/60ml of water around it.

Grill (broil) the fish for 8–10 minutes or until brown on top and cooked through. Baste a few times with the juices.

To assemble

Set up 4 warm plates. Divide the spinach into 4 and put a portion in the centre of each plate. Divide the fish in 4, carefully lifting up the portions and setting down on the spinach. Pour some tomato sauce over each piece of fish and serve immediately.

GINGERY CAULIFLOWER WITH GRATED CHEESE
Serves 4–6

I did not know until fairly recently that my grandmother was a vegetarian. You see, when she was alive and we lived together in Delhi, she sat at one end of a very long dining table and we, the little children, sat at the other end. We could all see our grandfather. He sat at the head of the table and he was tall. I could see quite clearly that he drank soda water with his meals (to aid digestion, we were told) and waved his white beard about as he spoke. My grandmother, who sat to his left, was short and somehow got lost amongst the protuberances of more imposing relatives. I could not see her plate, let alone what she was putting on it. Ten years ago, while visiting my oldest aunt, I found out. Whatever my grandmother was putting on her plate, I was told, it was *never* meat. I was also told that if I thought *I* was pretty clever in the kitchen, I should have seen my grandmother. Why, she *invented* 'Cauliflower with Cheese'. What sort of cheese, I wondered. My grandmother was so traditionally Indian. English cheese, I was told, from the English shop. New aspects of my grandmother emerged – and a new cross-cultural recipe! Here I have used grated Parmesan cheese instead of the 'English' cheese, which was probably a strong Cheddar.

5 tablespoons/75ml vegetable oil
1 teaspoon/5ml whole cumin seeds
2 teaspoons/10ml peeled and minced fresh ginger
¼ teaspoon cayenne pepper
4 teaspoons/20ml ground coriander seeds
¼ teaspoon ground turmeric
A medium-sized (1¾-lb/800-g) head of cauliflower, cut into small, slim florets
About ¾ teaspoon/4ml salt, or to taste
2 teaspoons/10ml lemon juice
4 tablespoons/60ml/¼ cup finely grated Parmesan cheese

Heat the oil in a wok or a large pan over a high flame. When hot, put in the cumin seeds. After a few seconds, put in the ginger. Stir once or twice. Now put in the cayenne, coriander and turmeric. Stir quickly and put in the cauliflower and salt. Stir the cauliflower for a minute. Add about 4floz/120ml/½ cup water, cover, and continue to cook on fairly high heat for about 5 minutes or until the cauliflower has just cooked through and the liquid has evaporated. Remove the cover, turn the heat down and add the lemon juice. Taste for seasonings. The cauliflower should be very slightly undersalted. Empty the cauliflower on to a serving dish. Sprinkle cheese over the top and toss. Serve immediately.

BOILED NEW POTATOES WITH ROSEMARY AND PARSLEY
Serves 4

New potatoes come in all sizes. I like the very small ones, no bigger than 1–1½in/2.5–4cm in diameter. I can usually find them only at our local farm markets. If you can get hold of them, allow about 5 or 6 per person. You could use small red potatoes as well. Allow about 4 per person. If you can only find large boiling potatoes, allow about 2 per person. Peel and then halve or quarter them before boiling.

New potatoes (see note above) scrubbed, but not peeled
Salt to taste
3 tablespoons/45ml olive oil
½ teaspoon/2.5ml fresh or ¼ teaspoon dried rosemary, very finely chopped
2 tablespoons/30ml finely chopped fresh parsley

Boil the potatoes in salted water until just tender. Drain. Heat the oil in a wide pot or large frying pan over a medium flame. When hot, put in the rosemary. Stir around for 30 seconds. Put in the parsley. Stir once and put in the potatoes. Stir gently until the potatoes are coated with oil and with the herbs. Serve hot.

ALL OF MY FAVOURITE THINGS

ARTICHOKES SERVED WITH GINGER BUTTER
GRILLED (BROILED) SALMON STEAKS WITH
MINTY YOGHURT SAUCE
RICE WITH ASPARAGUS

I love artichokes, fresh salmon and asparagus and so does every member of my family. There are times when we indulge ourselves totally and have them all at the same meal.

I do not much care for whole artichokes when they are icy cold, so even when I cook them in advance, I reheat them in a little water before serving. They are wonderful dipped in ginger-flavoured butter. I have everything ready for the rice and set it to cook about half an hour before we sit down to dinner. The salmon should be grilled (broiled) at the last minute, though part of its sauce – the tomato section of it – can be made in advance.

ARTICHOKES SERVED WITH GINGER BUTTER

Serves 6

I could live on artichokes. I discovered them rather late in life as I was sailing adventurously on the *Queen Mary* – alone and on my way to America for the very first time. I actually discovered three things on that historic journey: Bermuda shorts – which I did not care for (still don't); heart of iceberg lettuce, doused with a vinaigrette sauce – which I loved (and still do, so do not denounce it in my presence); and artichokes.

The artichokes were cooked very simply – just boiled and served with melted butter. I still love them that way and seem to have communicated this passion to my husband and children. We all sit around our dining table in New York, picking off leaf after leaf and pulling away the tender flesh with our teeth. Used-up leaves are dropped into a communal bowl in the centre of our round table. The level in the bowl keeps rising and we all wait to see who will offer to empty it. Given half a chance, nobody would stir. We nudge and suggest. No one can stop eating, that is the problem.

I sometimes flavour the melted butter with a little garlic, at other times with a few drops of ginger juice and lemon juice.

6 good-sized artichokes
6oz/115g/½ cup unsalted butter
2 teaspoons/10ml lemon juice
2 teaspoons/10ml very finely grated, peeled fresh ginger
Salt

Trim the artichokes: pull off the small leaves on the upper part of the stems. Cut the stems so they are level with the bottoms of the artichokes. With a sharp knife, cut off about 1in/2.5cm from the leaves at the top of the globe. With a pair of scissors, cut off the prickly tops of all the remaining leaves.

Bring a large pot of water to a boil. Drop in

Opposite

CLOCKWISE FROM THE TOP: ARTICHOKE WITH GINGER BUTTER, MINTY YOGHURT SAUCE, GRILLED (BROILED) SALMON STEAK SERVED WITH RICE AND ASPARAGUS

the artichokes – I wedge them in stem-down – cover, turn heat to medium-low, and boil for 15–20 minutes for medium-sized artichokes, 30–40 minutes for larger artichokes. They are done when an outer leaf pulls out easily. Drain thoroughly.

While the artichokes are cooking, melt the butter. Add the lemon juice. Now hold the grated ginger between your fingers and squeeze it, letting the juice from it run into the melted butter. Discard the ginger in your hand. Add a *very* tiny sprinkling of salt – about ¹⁄₁₆ teaspoon. Mix and taste for seasoning.

Put each drained artichoke on a plate. It should be hot or warm. Divide the melted butter into 6 small bowls. Put each bowl on a plate beside the artichoke and serve.

(Put one or more large bowls in the centre of the table for discarded leaves.)

GRILLED (BROILED) SALMON STEAKS WITH MINTY YOGHURT SAUCE

Serves 6

Because I wasn't raised in a salmon-producing region and because this fish is never cheap in New York, I have always considered it a very special treat. Whenever I wish to indulge myself or my family – and this happens all too often, I am afraid – I have my fishmonger cut me 3-in/8-cm wide pieces from a salmon fillet. If the fishmonger does not sell filleted salmon, I buy 3-in/8-cm thick steaks and have the butcher cut them in half, thus removing the central bone. I cook these steaks in many ways but perhaps the most refreshing way is this one.

You can easily serve more or fewer people by increasing or decreasing the number of steaks. The yoghurt sauce here will stretch even to 8 people.

For the Fish

6 3-in/8-cm wide pieces of salmon, cut from a side of salmon fillet (see note above)
About 2 tablespoons/30ml lemon juice
Salt
Freshly ground black pepper
Dash of cayenne pepper
1 teaspoon/5ml ground cumin seeds
About 2 tablespoons/30ml melted butter or olive oil

For the Sauce

1lb/450g red-ripe tomatoes
3 tablespoons/45ml olive oil
2 teaspoons/10ml whole yellow mustard seeds
1 spring onion (scallion), cut into very fine rings all the way up its green section
½–1 fresh hot green or red chilli, very finely chopped
¼ teaspoon dried thyme
4 well-packed tablespoons/60ml chopped fresh mint
Salt
Freshly ground black pepper
1½ pints/845ml/4 cups plain yoghurt at room temperature, beaten lightly until smooth and creamy

Lay the fish pieces, skin side down, in a grilling (broiling) tray. Sprinkle the lemon juice over them and spread it out evenly with your fingers. Sprinkle the salt, black pepper, cayenne, and cumin seeds over the top. Brush with melted butter or the oil. Set aside.

Bring a large pot of water to a boil. Drop in the tomatoes for 15 seconds. Drain. Peel the tomatoes and cut in half, crosswise. Hold one half in your hand, cut side down and gently squeeze out as many of the seeds as you can. Do that with all the halves. Now chop up the tomato shells into fairly small pieces.

Heat the 3 tablespoons/45ml olive oil in a frying pan over a medium-high flame. When hot, put in the mustard seeds. As soon as they begin to pop (this just takes a few seconds) put in the chopped tomatoes, spring onion (scallion), green or red chilli and thyme. Stir and cook for about 2 minutes or until the tomatoes have softened slightly. Add the mint and stir once or twice. Turn off heat. Add salt and pepper to taste. Keep warm (not boiling hot).

Preheat the grill (broiler).

Set water to boil in the bottom container of a double-boiler.

Put the fish under the grill (broiler). It will take 5–8 minutes, depending on its thickness. It should turn golden brown on the top and be cooked through.

Put the yoghurt in the top container of the double boiler. Add 1 teaspoon/5ml salt. Stir gently in one direction until the yoghurt is very warm. Add the warm yoghurt to the warm tomato mixture. Stir to mix.

To serve, either pass the sauce separately or, if serving on individual plates as I do, spoon a little of the sauce on top of the salmon piece and spoon a little more beside it. Any sauce that is left can always be passed around on the side.

RICE WITH ASPARAGUS

Serves 6

Here the asparagus lends its gentle aroma and its lovely green colour to the puffy white grains of rice, making this a delicate, exquisite dish.

Long-grain rice, measured to the 15-fl oz/425-ml/2 cup level in a glass measuring jug
1 lb/450g fresh asparagus of medium thickness
4 tablespoons/60ml olive oil
Salt
18fl oz/500ml/2⅓ cups chicken broth or stock, home-made or canned
2fl oz/55ml/⅓ cup dry white vermouth

Wash the rice in several changes of water. Drain. Cover with water and leave to soak for 30 minutes. Drain.

Meanwhile, trim and discard the coarser ends of the asparagus. Peel the lower half of the spears and then cut them into 1-in/2.5-cm pieces.

Heat the oil in a wide heavy pot over a medium flame. When hot, put in the asparagus. Stir and fry for 1½–2 minutes. Remove the asparagus with a slotted spoon and keep in a bowl. Put the rice into the same pot in the remaining oil. Stir and sauté for 2 minutes. Add the chicken broth, vermouth and about 1 teaspoon/5ml salt if using salted broth, 1½ teaspoons/7.5ml if using unsalted stock. Bring to a boil. Cover tightly, turn heat to very low, and simmer gently for 20 minutes.

Meanwhile, sprinkle the asparagus very lightly with salt and toss. When the rice has cooked for 20 minutes, quickly lift up the lid, put the asparagus and any juices that may have accumulated into the rice pot, cover again immediately and cook for another 5 minutes. Mix the rice gently before serving.

WAFTING THROUGH THE SUMMER

SUMMER YOGHURT AND GREEN PEA SOUP
GRILLED (BROILED) FISH WITH GARLIC AND TOMATO
BOILED NEW POTATOES WITH TURMERIC-CUMIN BUTTER
GREEN BEANS WITH MUSTARD AND GINGER

All one wants in the summer are light, cooling foods that are easy to prepare – simply grilled (broiled) fish, full of flavour and succulence, a chilled soup to precede it and a couple of well-chosen vegetables – new potatoes with an exotic hint of cumin and turmeric, and green beans flavoured with some refreshingly pungent ginger.

SUMMER YOGHURT AND GREEN PEA SOUP

Serves 4

This cooling, green summer soup, perfect for those warm days filled with the sound of bees buzzing around the lavender, is very light as well. It looks creamy, but its texture comes from low-fat yoghurt. It has mint in it as well as fresh green coriander (Chinese parsley) and peas, all of which you might well be able to pick from your kitchen garden or else buy easily, all fresh and crisp, from your local market.

It is strange how one keeps finding new and better ways to do old things. I used to tie whole spices in a cheesecloth pouch before dropping them into a simmering broth, in order to flavour it. When I was making this soup for the first time, I decided to flavour it with 2 teaspoons/10ml whole cumin seeds. This spice is considered to be particularly effective in cooling down the body. I looked around – no cheesecloth in sight. I could have looked for a clean rag or whatever, but instead I just reached out for a stainless steel tea-ball, the kind used for infusing tea, filled it with the seeds and dropped it into the simmering stock. How easy! I'll never do it any other way!

One other point. In case you have not already discovered it, electric blenders seem to purée vegetable soups much better than food processors. If you only have a food processor, strain out all the vegetables and try blending them just by themselves. Then slowly add the stock. You may still have to push the soup through a strainer to get it smooth.

1 medium-sized potato (3oz/85g), peeled and diced
1 small onion, peeled and chopped
2 teaspoons/10ml whole cumin seeds, tied in cheesecloth or put inside a tea-ball
A ½-in/1.5cm cube of peeled fresh ginger, chopped
1½ pints/845ml/4 cups chicken broth or stock (fresh or canned)
½ fresh hot green chilli, chopped (optional)
6½oz/195g/1½ cups shelled peas, fresh or frozen
1oz/30g/1 lightly packed cup chopped fresh green coriander (Chinese parsley)
12 good-sized fresh mint leaves

6fl oz/150ml/¾ cup low-fat yoghurt, blended until smooth with 4 tablespoons/60ml/¼ cup water
Salt to taste

Combine the potato, onion, cumin seeds, ginger, chicken broth and green chilli in a large pot and bring to a boil. Cover, lower the heat and simmer for 30 minutes. Lift the cover, remove the bag (or tea-ball) with the cumin seeds and put in the shelled peas. Bring to a boil. Turn the heat down and simmer for 2 minutes. Add the fresh green coriander (Chinese parsley) and mint leaves. Simmer for another minute. Turn off heat.

Empty the soup into the container of an electric blender and, in one or two batches, blend until it is smooth. Pour the soup into a clean bowl. Allow to cool. Add the yoghurt and mix. Taste for salt. Cover and chill in the refrigerator. Serve cold.

GRILLED (BROILED) FISH WITH GARLIC AND TOMATO

Serves 4

This dish tastes delightful and cooks very easily and quickly. I use red snapper fillets, but if you cannot find them, you may use sole or sea bass.

2 ¾lb/1.25kg (2 smallish) red snapper/sole/sea bass, heads removed and filleted
3 plum tomatoes from a can, chopped
Salt
Freshly ground black pepper
1 clove garlic, very finely chopped
½ fresh, hot green chilli, very finely chopped
3 tablespoons/45ml olive oil
1 tablespoon/15ml chopped fresh parsley

Preheat the grill (broiler). Lay the 4 fish pieces out in a grilling (broiling) tray, skin side down. Sprinkle the tomatoes, salt, black pepper, chopped garlic and hot chilli over the top. Dribble oil all along the lengths of the fish pieces. Grill (broil) for 7–8 minutes or until nicely browned on the top and cooked through. Baste now and then with the juices in the tray. Garnish with the parsley before serving.

BOILED NEW POTATOES WITH TURMERIC-CUMIN BUTTER

Serves 4–5

I try and get the smallest-sized new potatoes for this, those that are about 1in/2.5cm in diameter. Small red potatoes work equally well. Whatever size you get, boil them in their jackets until they are just tender, not mushy or split open.

2 lb/900g small potatoes (new or red potatoes are best)
2 tablespoons/30ml peanut, groundnut or corn oil
1 teaspoon/5ml whole cumin seeds
¼ teaspoon ground turmeric
2 tablespoons/30ml unsalted butter, cut into small pats
1 teaspoon/5ml salt
Freshly ground black pepper
¼ teaspoon cayenne pepper (optional)

Boil the potatoes in their jackets until just done. Drain and leave to cool. Heat the oil in a large wok or frying pan over a medium-high flame. When hot, put in the whole cumin seeds. Ten seconds later, put in the ground turmeric. Stir once quickly and put in the butter. Stir quickly once or twice. The butter should melt. Now put in the potatoes, salt, black pepper and cayenne. Stir the potatoes around for 1–2 minutes until well-coated with the butter and heated through. Serve hot.

GREEN BEANS WITH MUSTARD AND GINGER

Serves 4

These beans may be served hot, at room temperature or cold. They have a gentle, gingery pungence.

1 tablespoon/15ml Dijon-style mustard
1 tablespoon/15ml red wine vinegar
1 well-packed teaspoon/5ml peeled, finely grated fresh ginger
½ teaspoon/2.5ml salt – or to taste
Freshly ground black pepper
⅛–¼ teaspoon cayenne pepper
4 tablespoons/60ml olive oil
1½lb/675g green beans, trimmed at the ends but left whole

Set a large pot of water to boil.

Put the mustard in a small bowl. Add the vinegar, ginger, salt, pepper and cayenne. Mix. Slowly add the olive oil, beating it in with a fork as you do so.

Drop the beans into the boiling water. Boil rapidly for 3–5 minutes or until the beans are just cooked but still crisp. Drain thoroughly. Put the beans in a big bowl. Add the dressing and mix.

PERFUMED ORIENTAL DELIGHTS

RED PRAWNS (SHRIMP)
CUCUMBER IN A SOY DRESSING
PLAIN LONG-GRAIN RICE

I serve this colourful meal – with its red-sauced seafood, green cucumber salad and white rice – whenever I want a lunch or dinner that is both light and *very* easy to put together. It looks so pretty and tastes absolutely wonderful.

Very often, if friends are passing through New York or an agent or editor wants to come over to chat or a magazine is sending over a photographer, I will invite them to stay for lunch. With a minimum amount of organization I manage it so that I have to spend less than 10 minutes in the kitchen once my guests arrive. The prawn (shrimp) sauce can be made ahead of time, and the prawns (shrimp) peeled, washed, patted dry and refrigerated. The entire cucumber salad (with the exception of the final sprinkling of sesame seeds) may be made several hours in advance. As for the rice, I set it to soak about one hour before my guests arrive, and set it to cook about 30 minutes before the doorbell rings. If left covered in a warm spot, the rice stays hot for a good hour. This way, I can spend as much time as I like talking with my guests. Once it is time to eat, I throw the prawn (shrimp) dish together very quickly. The haunting aromas of prawns (shrimp), garlic and mustard seeds emanating from the kitchen stimulate appetites and serve as an indication to my guests to hasten to the dining table.

RED PRAWNS (SHRIMP)

Serves 4

I have borrowed techniques from both India and Indonesia to make this dish. In Indonesia, its redness comes from fresh hot red peppers. I use a combination of the sweet red pepper, paprika and a hint of cayenne instead. You may use scallops instead of prawns (shrimp).

1½lb/675g medium-sized prawns (shrimp)
1 whole fresh sweet red pepper
1 small onion, peeled and coarsely chopped
7 whole macadamia nuts (the bottled, roasted variety) or 10 raw cashew nuts
4 tablespoons/60ml vegetable oil
1 teaspoon/5ml yellow mustard seeds
2 cloves garlic, peeled and finely chopped
½ teaspoon/2.5ml cayenne pepper
1 teaspoon/5ml salt or to taste
1 teaspoon/5ml paprika

Peel and devein the prawns (shrimp). Wash, pat dry and set aside. Put the red pepper, onion and nuts into the container of a food processor. Blend thoroughly, stopping to push down ingredients with a rubber spatula whenever necessary. Take out the paste and keep in a bowl.

Heat 3 tablespoons/45ml of the oil in a wok or non-stick frying pan over a medium-high flame. When hot, put in the mustard seeds. As soon as the mustard seeds begin to pop, put in the garlic. Stir once and put in the prawns (shrimp). Sprinkle about ¼ teaspoon salt over the prawns (shrimp). Stir and fry for 2–3 minutes or until the prawns (shrimp) turn opaque. Remove them with a slotted spoon, leaving all the oil behind. Keep them in a bowl.

Add 1 tablespoon/15ml oil to the wok and put in the red pepper paste. Stir and fry for 4–5 minutes or until the sauce looks quite dry. Add the remaining ¼ teaspoon salt, the cayenne and paprika. Stir once and put in the prawns (shrimp), all the accumulated liquid from the bowl, and 4 tablespoons/60ml water. Lower heat and stir gently for 1 minute. You should have a very thick sauce. Serve immediately.

Overleaf

CLOCKWISE FROM THE TOP: CUCUMBER IN A SOY DRESSING, RED PRAWNS (SHRIMP), PLAIN LONG-GRAIN RICE

CUCUMBER IN A SOY DRESSING

Serves 4

I learned how to make this salad from two of my daughters who studied in Taiwan. Versions of it can be found all over China and Korea.

1¼ tablespoons/20ml sesame seeds
1¼lb/560g cucumbers, the pickling or English kind
3 tablespoons/45ml soy sauce
1 tablespoon plus 1 teaspoon/20ml distilled white vinegar
⅛ teaspoon cayenne pepper
½ teaspoon/2.5ml sugar
1 small clove garlic, peeled and well mashed
1 tablespoon/15ml oriental sesame oil or olive oil

Heat a small cast-iron frying pan or crêpe pan over a medium flame. When hot, put in the sesame seeds. Stir them around until they start to fly and smell roasted. Set aside.

Roll-cut the cucumbers this way: cut off and discard the ends. Make a diagonal slice at the end of the cucumber. Roll the cucumber 180° and make another diagonal slice. Continue until you have cut the cucumber into even-sized diamond-shaped chunks. Put in a shallow bowl, such as a soup bowl.

Combine the soy sauce, vinegar, sugar, cayenne, garlic and oil. Pour over the cucumbers. Set aside for 30 minutes (longer will not hurt), turning them occasionally to flavour and colour them evenly. Sprinkle the roasted sesame seeds over the top just before serving.

PLAIN LONG-GRAIN RICE

Serves 4–5

Long-grain rice measured to the 15-fl oz/425-ml/2 cup level in a glass measuring jug

Put the rice in a bowl and wash in several changes of water. Drain. Cover well with fresh water and set aside for 25 minutes or longer. Drain again.

Put the rice in a pot. Add 1pt/570ml/2⅔ cups water and bring to a boil. Cover tightly and turn heat to very, very low. Cook for 25 minutes.

ENTERTAINING WITH EASE

PRAWNS (SHRIMP) IN A PINK SAUCE
RICE WITH PEAS AND CARROTS, FLAVOURED
WITH CARDAMOM
SALAD OF WATERCRESS AND SEASONED APPLE

Without a doubt, this is one of my favourite meals, excellent both as lunch and dinner. The prawns (shrimp) have a spicy, creamy sauce, just perfect to be soaked up by the forkful with cardamom-flavoured rice. No vegetables are needed, as the rice dish is really a sort of casserole, containing both peas and carrots. A crisp salad, preferably one that has fruit in it, is all that is needed to finish off the meal. The rice will stay hot for a good hour after it is cooked, provided that it is kept covered in a warm place. All the ingredients for the prawn (shrimp) sauce may be assembled and mixed up to a day ahead, covered and refrigerated. I serve the salad after the prawn (shrimp) rice course.

I often serve the two main courses on this menu, separately, as first courses at other meals. Four or five of the prawns (shrimp) may be floated in a sea of sauce on small plates and the rice may be offered as one might an Italian risotto.

PRAWNS (SHRIMP) IN A PINK SAUCE

Serves 6

This dish is of Indian parentage. It did, originally, have rather a long list of ingredients. Once, when asked to cut it down somewhat for a national morning television programme, I discovered, to my great pleasure, that the dish suffered little and still tasted amazingly good. It is very easy to make.

For the Sauce

4 tablespoons/60ml tomato purée mixed with enough water to make 8fl oz/237ml/1 cup tomato sauce
8fl oz/237ml/1 cup single (heavy) cream
1½ teaspoons/7.5ml finely grated, peeled fresh ginger
¼ teaspoon cayenne pepper (add more, if desired)
4 teaspoons/20ml lemon juice
1 teaspoon/5ml ground cumin seeds
About 1 teaspoon/5ml salt, or to taste
A little freshly ground black pepper
½ teaspoon/2.5ml sugar

You Also Need

3 tablespoons/45ml olive or other vegetable oil
1 tablespoon/15ml whole yellow mustard seeds
2 cloves garlic, peeled and finely chopped
2 lb/900g medium-sized prawns (shrimp), peeled and deveined
Salt and freshly ground black pepper

Mix all the ingredients for the sauce. Cover and refrigerate until needed. (This may be done up to a day in advance.)

Five minutes before you sit down to eat, heat the oil in a large frying pan over a medium-high flame. When hot, put in the mustard seeds. As soon as the mustard seeds begin to pop (this takes just a few seconds), put in the garlic. Stir once and put in the prawns (shrimp). Stir and fry until the prawns (shrimp) just turn opaque, sprinkling them lightly with salt and pepper as you do so. Pour in the sauce and stir. As soon as the sauce starts bubbling, the dish is ready to be served.

RICE WITH PEAS AND CARROTS, FLAVOURED WITH CARDAMOM

Serves 6

This pilaf has Indo-Persian roots and is quite scrumptious. It might not be a bad idea to remove the large whole spices before you serve, as they are not meant to be eaten.

Long-grain rice, measured to the 15-fl oz/425-ml/2 cup level in a glass measuring jug
2 medium-sized carrots
3 tablespoons/45ml vegetable oil
3 whole cardamom pods
A 1-in/2.5-cm stick of cinnamon
4 whole cloves
Half a medium-sized onion, peeled and cut into fine half-rings
1 pint/570ml/2½ cups chicken broth or stock, fresh or canned
Salt
6oz/175g/1¼ cups shelled peas, fresh or frozen (if frozen, defrost first in warm water)

Put the rice in a bowl and wash in several changes of water. Drain. Cover well with fresh water and leave to soak for 25 minutes or longer. Drain and leave in a strainer set over a bowl.

Peel the carrots, trim them and cut them into sticks. Cut the sticks into ¼-in/6-mm dice.

Heat the oil in a heavy medium-sized pot over a medium-high flame. When hot, put in the cardamom, cinnamon and cloves. Stir once or twice and put in the onion. Stir and fry until the onion browns a bit. Put in the carrots. Stir and fry for a minute. Put in the drained rice. Continue to stir and fry, turning the heat down slightly if the rice seems to stick, for 2 minutes or until the rice turns translucent and is nicely coated with the oil. Pour in the broth, adding 1½ teaspoons/7.5ml salt if it is unsalted, ¾ teaspoon/4ml if it is salted. Bring to a boil. Cover, turn heat to very low and cook for 20 minutes. Lift the cover, quickly put in the peas, cover again and cook for another 5–10 minutes or until the peas are tender. Mix gently before serving.

SALAD OF WATERCRESS AND SEASONED APPLE

Serves 6

The roasted and ground cumin seeds used in this recipe are a flavouring I use in many of my dishes, so I make up a quantity at a time and keep it handy in the kitchen. To make, heat a small cast-iron frying pan over a medium flame; put in 4 tablespoons/60ml or more of whole cumin seeds, and stir and cook them till they turn a few shades darker and emit a wonderful roasted aroma. Let the seeds cool a bit in a dish, then grind as finely as possible in a spice grinder or clean coffee grinder. Store in a tightly lidded jar.

1 hard, medium-sized crisp apple (such as a Granny Smith)
1 tablespoon/15ml lemon juice
Salt
Freshly ground black pepper
⅛ teaspoon ground roasted cumin seeds (see note above)
Dash of cayenne pepper
¼ teaspoon sugar
5 teaspoons/25ml olive oil
2 bunches watercress (store weight about 10oz/285g)
4 teaspoons/20ml red wine vinegar
4 teaspoons/20ml soy sauce

Peel and quarter the apple. Core the quarters and then cut each slice, lengthwise, into 7–8 thin slices. Put in a bowl and rub with the lemon juice. Add about ¼ teaspoon salt, black pepper, cumin, cayenne, sugar, and 1 teaspoon/5ml of the olive oil. Rub gently to mix. Arrange the slices prettily in the centres of six salad plates and set aside.

Trim the watecress, removing all coarse stems. Wash and pat dry.

Just before serving, put the watercress in a bowl. Add the vinegar, soy sauce, and the remaining 4 teaspoons/20ml olive oil. Sprinkle some black pepper over the top. Toss and taste for salt. Put on top of the apple slices and serve.

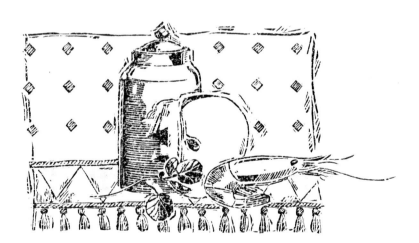

CHOOSING CHICKEN

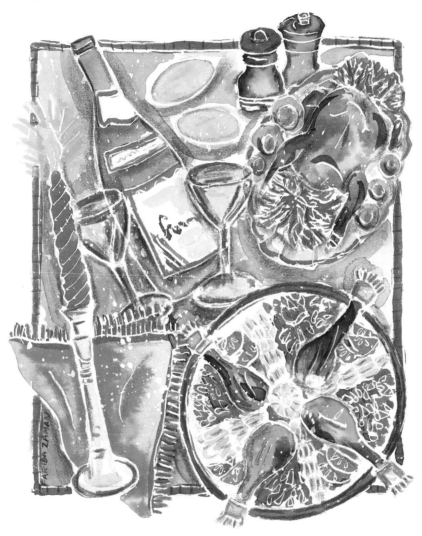

COOKING WITHOUT FUSS

ARTICHOKES IN BROTH
PASTA WITH CHICKEN LIVERS AND TOMATO SAUCE
LETTUCE AND STRAWBERRY SALAD

When I want friends to drop in for dinner, and do not want to spend all day cooking, this is what I make. I often cook the same dinner for our family as well. The meal has three things we all dote on – artichokes, pasta and strawberries.

The very process of plucking off the leaves of the artichokes draws out the meal and gives it an easy, leisured pace.

The artichokes are followed by a comforting and scumptious pasta dish. The last item, a green salad with strawberries, is as unusual as it is good, and can easily take the place of dessert.

ARTICHOKES IN BROTH

Serves 4

Here is my simplified version of a delightful Italian dish. The broth serves as a dipping sauce. This dish may be made ahead of time and reheated.

I serve this dish in individual old-fashioned soup plates, the artichoke sitting magnificently in a sea of parsley-flecked broth. I rarely bother to trim away the tips of the leaves for this recipe.

4 medium to large artichokes
1½ pints/845ml/4 cups chicken broth or stock, freshly made or canned
4 tablespoons/60ml olive oil
2 well-packed teacups of chopped fresh flat-leaf Italian parsley (use ordinary parsley as a substitute)
1 medium-sized onion, peeled and chopped
3 cloves garlic, peeled and chopped
Salt to taste if needed
Freshly ground black pepper

Wash the artichokes well and trim the stems.

Put the chicken broth in a pot wide enough to accommodate the 4 artichokes. Add the olive oil, parsley, onion, garlic, salt if needed, and black pepper. Bring to a simmer, turn down heat and simmer for 5 minutes.

Put the artichokes, stem side down, in the liquid. Ladle a little liquid on the tops of the artichokes. Bring to a boil. Cover, turn heat to low and simmer for 20–30 minutes or until an outside leaf pulls away easily. Lift up an artichoke at a time and place in the centre of a soup plate. Ladle the broth around it. Serve hot.

PASTA WITH CHICKEN LIVERS AND TOMATO SAUCE

Serves 4–5

There are two members of our family (*and* a boyfriend of one of these two members) who profess to loathe chicken livers, but not this dish, it seems. They insist it is because the chicken livers are chopped up and rendered invisible! At any rate, this is a very popular dish at home and a cheap one at that. The pasta I use is fusilli (the corkscrews) though you could use linguini if you so wished. This dish is prepared in several pots. You may, if you wish, prepare the tomato sauce well ahead of time and either refrigerate or freeze it. It should be reheated before serving. Almost everything that requires chopping may be got ready in advance, but should be cooked just after the pasta goes into a pot of boiling water.

For the Tomato Sauce

4 tablespoons/60ml olive oil
5 cloves garlic, peeled and chopped
1 medium-sized onion, peeled and chopped
A 28-oz/800-g can of whole tomatoes, chopped coarsely
¼ teaspoon dried thyme
1 teaspoon/5ml dried oregano
1 bay leaf
1 whole dried hot red pepper (optional)
1¼ teaspoons/6.25ml salt – or to taste
Freshly ground black pepper

You Also Need

1¼lb/560g fusilli
Salt
5 tablespoons/75ml olive oil
3 spring onions (scallions), sliced all the way up the green section
A quarter of a sweet red pepper, cut into ⅛-in/3-mm dice
10 medium-sized mushrooms, sliced
½lb/225g chicken livers, chopped into ¼-in/6-mm dice
A generous pinch of dried sage
A generous pinch of dried thyme
3 tablespoons/45ml red wine

The tomato sauce

Heat the oil in a pot over a medium flame. When hot, put in the garlic and onion. Sauté until the onion has wilted. Now put in the chopped-up tomatoes, the remaining juice in the can, as well as all the other ingredients for the sauce. Bring to a simmer. Cook, uncovered, on a medium-low flame for 20 minutes or so or until the sauce is no longer watery. Cover and keep warm.

Time the cooking of the pasta so it is ready just before it is to be eaten. Cook the pasta according to package directions in lots of salted boiling water. Do not overcook.

While it is cooking, heat 3 tablespoons/45ml of the olive oil in a frying pan over a medium-high flame. Put in the spring onions (scallions) and red pepper and stir until they are slightly wilted. Now put in the mushrooms. Stir and fry until mushrooms are just wilted. Add about ¼ teaspoon salt. Stir to mix and taste to check the salt. Empty the contents of the pan into a bowl.

Heat the remaining 2 tablespoons/30ml of oil in the same pan over a highish flame. When hot, put in the chopped livers, sage, thyme and a scant ½ teaspoon/2.5ml of salt. Stir on high heat until livers are lightly browned and just done – this does not take long. Remove the livers with a slotted spoon and put in a clean bowl. Add the wine to the frying pan. Lower heat a bit and scrape up all the pan juices. Pour these over the liver. Quickly set about assembling the pasta. Drain the pasta and put in a very large shallow bowl or dish. Spoon the tomato sauce over the top. On top of the sauce, spread out the mushroom mixture, and on top of that, the chopped liver. Bring to the table, toss and serve.

LETTUCE AND STRAWBERRY SALAD
Serves 4

Ever since childhood, I have enjoyed eating fruit that has a hint of tartness to it with a pinch of salt – oranges, apples, pomegranates, all have been devoured that way. My mother often made 'salads' for us at lunchtime with guavas or peaches, smothering them with salt, pepper, cayenne, cumin and lime juice.

I happened one summer to be in England during the Wimbledon – and hence the strawberry – season. I was playing *Medea* at the Lyric Theatre in Hammersmith and chose to fortify myself before matinées with light repasts. One could hardly fly around the stage murdering children if one was weighed down by a full stomach. So I stuck to salads.

One particular day, I opened the refrigerator and found that all it contained was strawberries (left over from a previous binge that included chewy meringues and double cream) and some lettuce. I threw the two together in a bowl, added a simple dressing and found myself eating a divine salad.

Now, I often serve this as a last course, thus combining salad and dessert.

The Dressing

1 teaspoon/5ml Dijon-style mustard
2 tablespoons/30ml wine vinegar
½ teaspoon/2.5ml salt – or to taste
Freshly ground black pepper
4fl oz/120ml/½ cup olive oil

You Also Need

About 18 medium-sized strawberries, washed, hulled and split in half, lengthwise
1 head of any lettuce of your choice – I like the crisp inner leaves of cos (romaine), washed, patted dry, and torn into pieces

Put the mustard in a small bowl, add the vinegar, salt and black pepper. Mix. Slowly beat in the oil until it is absorbed and the dressing is creamy. Put the strawberries and lettuce in a serving bowl. Add as much of the dressing as you think you need to moisten the salad. Toss and serve.

Previous Page
CLOCKWISE FROM THE TOP: LETTUCE AND STRAWBERRY SALAD, PASTA WITH CHICKEN LIVERS AND TOMATO SAUCE, ARTICHOKES IN BROTH

SHADES OF ANGLO-INDIA

GINGERY CHICKEN BREASTS
FRIED POTATOES FLAVOURED WITH FENNEL SEEDS
STEWED GREEN BEANS FLAVOURED WITH FRESH GREEN
CORIANDER (CHINESE PARSLEY)

Where I was growing up in British India, it was not uncommon to have cooks we called *khansamahs* or 'lords of the household' who were trained in both classical Moghul dishes (delicate pilafs, lamb braised in yoghurt) and so-called 'English' ones ('roly-poly' – a jelly roll with a custard sauce, roast lamb with mint sauce). They also produced a third kind of food – today we would call it 'East-West food' – that took elements from each cuisine and combined them to produce delicately pungent meals. These would please both English masters who were looking for something 'exotic' but did not want to be overwhelmed with hot spices, and Indian masters, also looking for something 'exotic' – perhaps 'English' chops or cutlets which they could sit down to eat rather grandly with their Sheffield knives and forks, doing the entire soup-to-pudding routine with pomp if not splendour. Since Indians have a fairly low tolerance for *very* bland foods, a little ginger and garlic, maybe cumin as well, was invariably added to give the dull English foods a bit of pep – a trick these *khansamahs* discovered delighted both their English and their Indian employers.

This meal is very much part of that Anglo-Indian tradition. Chicken breast 'cutlets' are delicately perked up with ginger, the stewed green beans have hot pepper, garlic and fresh green coriander (Chinese parsley) to give them interest and the potatoes are fried in fennel-flavoured oil. It happens to be a delicious combination and one that is quick and easy to prepare. The potatoes can be boiled up to a day ahead of time. The green beans can be stewed at one's convenience and then reheated. The chicken requires a half-hour marination, but it takes less than 5 minutes to cook. It is best to start the potatoes frying first – they take about 15 minutes – and then do the chicken when they are almost ready.

GINGERY CHICKEN BREASTS

Serves 6

This is not only a favourite with our family, but a dish our daughters often cook themselves when they are entertaining their friends. It is simple to make and tastes quite scrumptious.

5 cloves garlic, peeled and mashed to a pulp
2 teaspoons/10ml peeled and very finely grated fresh ginger
¼–½ teaspoon/1.25–2.5ml cayenne pepper (optional)
1 tablespoon/15ml ground cumin seeds
1½ teaspoons/7.5ml salt
Freshly ground black pepper
2½ tablespoons/37ml distilled white vinegar
3 whole chicken breasts, separated into 6 halves, skinned, boned and flattened (the butcher can do this), each about ½in/1.5cm thick
3 tablespoons/45ml olive or other vegetable oil
2 tablespoons/30ml finely chopped chives or chopped parsley

Put the garlic, ginger, cayenne, cumin, salt, pepper and vinegar in a small bowl. Mix well. This is the marinade.

Put the chicken in a larger bowl. Empty the marinade over it and mix well. Prod all pieces lightly with a fork, so the marinade goes inside a bit. (Do not let the pieces break; handle them gently.) Set aside for half an hour.

Heat 2 tablespoons/30ml of the oil in a non-stick frying pan over a medium-high flame. When hot, pat the chicken pieces with paper towels and put in as many as the pan will hold in a single layer. Cook for 2–3 minutes or until nicely browned. Turn over and brown the second sides for another 2–3 minutes. The chicken should be just cooked through. Put on a warm serving plate. Do the other chicken pieces the same way, adding the extra tablespoon of oil to the pan as and when you need it. Garnish with the chives or parsley and serve hot.

FRIED POTATOES FLAVOURED WITH FENNEL SEEDS

Serves 6

2 lb/900g boiling potatoes
Enough vegetable oil to have about ⅛in/3mm in the bottom of a large frying pan
1 teaspoon/5ml whole fennel seeds
½ teaspoon/2.5ml bright red paprika
⅛–¼ teaspoon cayenne pepper (optional)
Salt
Freshly ground black pepper

Boil the potatoes and let them cool completely. Peel them and then cut them into half lengthwise.

Heat the oil in a large frying pan over a medium flame. When very hot, put in the fennel seeds. A second later, put in the potatoes, cut side down, in a single layer. (If one pan is not large enough, use two.) Let the potatoes turn a rich reddish-brown colour on the bottom. Turn them over and brown the second side. Just before the second side is done, sprinkle with paprika and cayenne pepper. Remove the potatoes with a slotted spoon and drain on paper towels. Dust with salt and freshly ground pepper. Serve hot and crisp.

STEWED GREEN BEANS FLAVOURED WITH FRESH GREEN CORIANDER (CHINESE PARSLEY)

Serves 6

This dish may be made up to a day ahead of time and then reheated.

---
3 tablespoons/45ml olive or other vegetable oil

1 dried hot red pepper (optional)

2 medium-sized onions, peeled, halved lengthwise, and then cut into fine half-rings

4 cloves garlic, peeled and finely chopped

1 lb/450g red-ripe tomatoes, peeled (after dropping into boiling water for 15 seconds first) and chopped, or 7–8 canned plum tomatoes, chopped

---

1½lb/675g green beans, trimmed and cut into 2in/5cm lengths

1½ teaspoons/7.5ml salt, or to taste

Freshly ground black pepper

4 tablespoons/60ml finely chopped fresh green coriander (Chinese parsley)

Heat the oil in a wide pot over a medium-high flame. When hot, put in the red pepper and stir once. Put in the garlic and onion. Turn heat to medium. Stir and fry until garlic and onion turn light brown at the edges. Put in the tomatoes, green beans, salt, black pepper, green coriander (Chinese parsley) and 4 tablespoons/60ml water. Bring to a simmer. Cover tightly, lower heat and simmer gently for 20 minutes or until beans are tender. Remove lid, raise heat and reduce the liquid to a thick sauce. Taste for salt. Remove red pepper before serving.

THE ELEGANCE OF THE MIDDLE EAST

GRILLED (BROILED) CHICKEN KEBABS
STIR-FRIED WATERCRESS
BULGAR WHEAT SALAD

Kebabs originated in the Middle East, and because of the ease of their preparation and their delicious flavour, quickly spread through much of southern Asia. Little cubes of meat and poultry, all nicely marinated and skewered, grill (broil) with such pleasing speed. New and fresh marinades are so easy to invent. The one I have used here borrows as much from North India as it does from Iran.

This kebab meal makes for an unusually pretty and colourful plate. The creamy white kebabs are alternated on the skewer with bits of sweet red pepper and, the way I serve it, they sit on a shimmering green bed of stir-fried watercress. On the side is a crunchy green and beige 'salad' of bulgar wheat and parsley. The watercress dish is actually of Chinese origin, but it goes so well with the kebabs that I have no hesitation whatsoever in inserting it into this very elegant Middle Eastern menu.

The bulgar wheat salad may be made ahead of time. You should also marinate the chicken, salt the watercress and cut up the red peppers as well as the seasoning for the watercress in advance. Then all you have to do at the last minute is place the kebabs under the grill and while they cook, stir-fry the watercress – which takes about 2 minutes or less. It is such a painless meal to prepare and so delicious to eat.

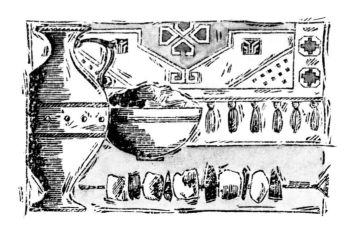

GRILLED (BROILED) CHICKEN KEBABS
Serves 4

These chicken kebabs are light, velvety and scrumptious – and so easy to make. I thread them with sweet red peppers because I like their colour and flavour. You may use sweet green peppers if you so prefer.

I make these kebabs under my grill (broiler). You may, if you like, cook them outdoors over a charcoal fire.

2 whole, skinned and boned chicken breasts (about 12oz/340g in all)
¾ teaspoon/4ml salt
3 tablespoons/45ml lemon juice
1 clove garlic, peeled and crushed to a pulp
1 teaspoon/5ml peeled and finely grated fresh ginger
¼ teaspoon ground allspice
¼ teaspoon ground nutmeg
Freshly ground black pepper
4 tablespoons/60ml single (heavy) cream
2 tablespoons/30ml olive oil
1 fresh sweet red pepper

Cut the chicken into 1¼-in/3-cm chunks and put in a bowl. Add the salt and lemon juice. Mix and set aside for 20–30 minutes. Now add the garlic, ginger, allspice, nutmeg, black pepper and the cream. Mix, cover and set aside in the refrigerator for 1–3 hours.

Preheat the grill (broiler).

Cut the red pepper into 1-in/2.5-cm squares, discarding all the seeds.

Divide the chicken into 4 portions. Thread one piece of red pepper on to a skewer, followed by 2 pieces of meat (long, thin pieces of meat may be doubled up), another piece of pepper and so on, until one portion of meat is used up. You should end with a piece of red pepper. Make up 4 skewers this way, brush them with oil and put them under the grill (broiler), about 4in/10cm from the source of heat. Cook for 2 minutes or until lightly browned. Keep turning, cooking each of the 4 sides for about 2–2½ minutes. The entire grilling (broiling) process should take about 10 minutes. Serve immediately.

STIR-FRIED WATERCRESS
Serves 4

Watercress can be good for more than just salads. It is a superb cooked vegetable as well. Here is a simple but quite delicious way to prepare it. It can be eaten hot or cold and retains its fresh green colour.

2 bunches watercress (10oz/285g in all)
1 teaspoon/5ml salt
2 tablespoons/30ml vegetable oil
1 clove garlic, peeled and finely chopped
¼ teaspoon peeled and finely chopped fresh ginger
1 tablespoon/15ml oriental sesame oil
Freshly ground black pepper

Chop the watercress finely, stems and all. Put in a bowl. Add the salt. Mix well, rubbing the salt in with your fingers. Set aside for 45 minutes. Squeeze out most of the moisture by picking up a handful at a time and pressing down on it with the other palm.

Heat the vegetable oil in a wok or frying pan over a high flame. When very hot, put in the garlic and ginger. Stir and fry for a few seconds. Now put in the watercress. Stir and fry for a minute or until the watercress just begins to soften. Add the sesame oil and the black pepper. Stir for about 10 seconds and serve.

BULGAR WHEAT SALAD
Serves 4

I love the nutty taste of bulgar – or cracked – wheat. As this refreshing salad requires no cooking it is simplicity itself to put together. Bulgar is sold in most supermarkets and all health food stores. You should get the fine-grain variety, as that is best for salads.

2 spring onions (scallions)
Fine bulgar wheat measured to the 8-fl oz/237-ml level in a glass measuring jug
2 loosely packed cups finely chopped fresh parsley
3 tablespoons/45ml lemon juice
3 tablespoons/45ml olive oil
Salt
Freshly ground black pepper
A few crisp leaves from a head of cos (romaine) lettuce

Cut the spring onions (scallions) into very fine rings all the way up their green sections. Soak in cold water for 45 minutes. Drain and gently squeeze out all the moisture. Pat dry.

Soak the bulgar wheat in plenty of water for 45 minutes. Drain. Take a handful of bulgar at a time, press down with the other palm and squeeze out as much water as possible. Put the squeezed bulgar in a bowl. Add the spring onions (scallions), parsley, lemon juice, olive oil, about ¾ teaspoon/4ml salt, and the pepper. Mix well and taste for seasonings, adding more salt if it is needed. Arrange on a plate or platter over a bed of lettuce leaves.

CLOCKWISE FROM THE TOP: STIR-FRIED WATER-CRESS, BULGAR WHEAT SALAD, GRILLED (BROILED) CHICKEN KEBABS

AROMATIC AND LIGHT

CHICKEN WITH HERBS

BROCCOLI RABE (OR BROCCOLI) WITH GARLIC AND
MUSTARD SEEDS

RICE WITH TOMATO AND MUSHROOMS

If you smother skinned chicken pieces with herbs and plain yoghurt, leave them marinating overnight, and then bake them quickly in a very hot oven, the results are delightful – and very light, perfect for the summer when you want to spend as little time in the kitchen as possible. The broccoli provides a healthy dash of greenery, while the rice with tomatoes gives the meal body, texture and an earthy flavour. The entire meal cooks within an hour and is a favourite with our family.

CHICKEN WITH HERBS

Serves 6

Here is a very refreshing chicken dish that is ideal for both invited friends and the family. It is simple to make, but does require an overnight marination. You can marinate the chicken up to two days in advance. Its flavour only improves. Those on diets should note that no fat is used in the cooking – even the skin of the chicken is discarded.

4 lb/1.8kg chicken parts (I use legs and breasts)
1½ teaspoons/7.5ml salt
1½ juicy lemons
1 small onion, peeled and chopped
1–2 fresh, hot green chillies
1 clove garlic, peeled
1 teaspoon/5ml peeled and finely grated fresh ginger
2 teaspoons/10ml ground cumin seeds
2 teaspoons/10ml dried thyme
2 teaspoons/10ml dried oregano
8fl oz/237ml/1 cup plain yoghurt
4 tablespoons/60ml finely chopped fresh parsley

Pull the skin off the chicken pieces by using a piece of paper towel to grip it firmly. Cut each leg into 2 and each breast into 4 pieces. Cut two parallel diagonal slits on each side of each part of the legs. The slits should never start at an edge and they should be deep enough to reach the bone. Cut similar slits on the meaty side of each breast piece.

Spread the chicken pieces out in a single layer on a large plate or plastic tray. Sprinkle evenly with half the salt. Sprinkle half of the juice from the lemons over the chicken and rub it in with your fingers. Now turn the chicken pieces over and do the same on the other side with remaining salt and lemon juice. Set aside for 20 minutes.

Meanwhile, in the container of a food processor or blender, combine the onion, green chillies, garlic, ginger, cumin, thyme, oregano and yoghurt. Blend until smooth.

Put the chicken and all accumulated juices in a bowl. Pour the marinade over it. Rub the marinade into the slits. Cover and refrigerate overnight or longer, turning the pieces over a few times.

Half an hour or so before eating, preheat the oven to its highest temperature. Meanwhile, spread the chicken out in a single layer in a shallow grilling (broiling) tray. Bake for 10 minutes on one side. Turn the chicken pieces over and bake for about 10 minutes on the other side or until the chicken is just done.

Arrange the chicken pieces on a warm serving plate. Sprinkle parsley generously over the top.

BROCCOLI RABE (OR BROCCOLI) WITH GARLIC AND MUSTARD SEEDS
Serves 6

Broccoli rabe is a green leafy vegetable that my husband and I just adore. If you've never tried it, you should. It has a deliciously bitter edge to it. If you cannot find it in your neighbourhood, you can substitute broccoli or even greens. I steam the vegetable first and then, just before eating, sauté it quickly in olive oil.

2 lb/900g broccoli rabe
5 tablespoons/75ml olive oil
2 teaspoons/10ml yellow mustard seeds
2–3 cloves garlic, peeled and finely chopped
Salt to taste

Trim away the coarse stalk ends of the vegetable. (In the case of broccoli, cut further into equal-sized slim spears, peeling the stalk when necessary.)

Set up your equipment for steaming. I just heat water in a large pot and balance a colander inside it. Cover and steam the broccoli rabe over high heat for 7–8 minutes or until it is just tender. (Broccoli will cook faster and should remain crisp-tender.) Remove from heat and rinse immediately under cold water to set the colour.

Just before eating, heat the oil in a frying pan over a medium-high flame. When hot, put in the mustard seeds. They will start popping. Now put in the garlic and stir once. Put in the broccoli and about ½ teaspoon/2.5ml salt, stirring gently to mix. Sauté for about a minute or until heated through and glistening. Serve immediately.

RICE WITH TOMATO AND MUSHROOMS
Serves 6

2 tablespoons/30ml vegetable oil
1 small (2-oz/60-g) onion, peeled and finely chopped
4 medium-sized mushrooms, wiped with a damp cloth and finely chopped
1 medium-sized (5-oz/140-g) tomato, finely chopped
Long-grain rice, measured to the 15-fl oz/ 425-ml/2 cup level in a glass measuring jug
1 teaspoon/5ml salt

Heat the oil in a heavy medium-sized pot over a high flame. When hot, put in the onion. Stir and fry until the onion is lightly browned. Put in the mushrooms. Stir and fry for a minute. Put in the tomato. Stir and fry for a minute. Put in the rice and salt. Continue to stir and fry for a minute. Now add 1 pint/570ml/2⅔ cups water and bring to a boil. Cover very tightly, turn heat to very low, and cook for 25 minutes.

CHICKEN 'N' SPICE 'N' EVERYTHING NICE

GRILLED (BROILED) CORIANDER-HONEY CHICKEN
HOT SWEET AND SOUR PEANUT SAUCE
TASTY GREEN BEANS WITH SOY SAUCE DRESSING
YELLOW RICE WITH CARROTS, RAISINS AND SESAME SEEDS

I remember once going to see a play that was set in the Hamptons on Long Island. An assortment of young people were sharing a house by the sea, each taking turns at the cooking. At one point, a character came in to announce that dinner was ready. When she informed the others that what she had cooked was grilled (broiled) chicken, they all let out a loud chorus of very pained groans.

I did not understand why.

Grilled (broiled) chicken can be so wonderful – moist inside, crackling crisp on the outside, and flavoured with all manner of seasonings and marinades, from a French blend of lavender-scented Provençal herbs to an oriental mix containing soy sauce and garlic.

This chicken dinner, a great favourite with our family, draws its inspiration (and its cooking techniques) from several countries, chiefly India, China and Indonesia. The chicken is slightly pungent, slightly sweet and slightly hot. It is served with a dollop of fiery peanut sauce. The green beans – Szechuan-style in the use of garlic and red pepper – complement the chicken perfectly, adding both a crunchy texture and some welcome greenery. The yellow rice completes a pretty balance of colours, and gives the meal a delicious nuttiness. It is a dinner you will want to make again and again.

GRILLED (BROILED) CORIANDER-HONEY CHICKEN

Serves 6

We make many versions of this chicken at home, the spices changing sufficiently each time for the family to describe them as the 'somewhat Japanese' version, the 'somewhat Chinese' version, and the 'somewhat Indonesian' version. This is the 'somewhat Indonesian' one and quite superb it is too. I have served it here as a dinner dish, but it is also quite good cold, taken along on a picnic. In the summer, this chicken may be grilled outdoors, with special care being taken not to let it char.

4 lb/1.8kg chicken parts (legs and breasts preferred)
6 tablespoons/90ml soy sauce
1–2 cloves garlic, peeled and mashed to a pulp
2 teaspoons/10ml finely grated peeled fresh ginger
1 tablespoon/15ml ground coriander seeds
¼ teaspoon ground turmeric
¼ teaspoon cayenne pepper (add more or less according to taste)
1 tablespoon/15ml honey

Cut each whole chicken leg into 2 pieces and each breast into 4. Cut two long, parallel, diagonal slits on each side of each leg piece. The slits should never start at an edge and should be deep enough to reach the bone. Cut similar slits on the meaty side of each breast piece. In a large bowl, combine the soy sauce, garlic, ginger, coriander, cayenne and honey. Mix until smooth. Put the chicken in this marinade. Rub marinade into all the pieces, making sure it goes deep into the slits. Set aside for 1–2 hours, turning the pieces now and then.

Preheat the grill (broiler) to a medium-high temperature (about 450°F/230°C/Gas Mark 8 is best).

Arrange the chicken pieces, skin side down, in a single layer in a grilling (broiling) tray. Cook for 12–15 minutes or until nicely browned, basting once with the juices. Turn the pieces over and cook the second side for another 12–15 minutes, basting once or twice with the juices. The chicken should be well browned.

HOT SWEET AND SOUR PEANUT SAUCE

Serves 6

4 tablespoons/60ml peanut butter (freshly made unsalted peanut butter from a health food store is best)
4 tablespoons/60ml soy sauce
1 tablespoon/15ml granulated brown sugar
2 tablespoons/30ml lemon juice
1½ teaspoons/7.5ml cayenne pepper or to taste

Combine all the ingredients and mix well. Serve in a small bowl as you would mustard or horseradish.

TASTY GREEN BEANS WITH SOY SAUCE DRESSING

Serves 6

1½lb/675g green beans, trimmed at the ends
3 tablespoons/45ml soy sauce
1 teaspoon/5ml sugar
1 tablespoon/15ml oriental sesame oil
3 tablespoons/45ml peanut, groundnut or other vegetable oil
6 cloves garlic, peeled and chopped
1 dried, hot red pepper, crumbled
Salt

Bring a large pot of water to a rolling boil. Drop in the beans and cook rapidly for 4–5 minutes or until just crisp-tender. Drain, and if not serving very soon, rinse under cold water. Leave to drain in a colander.

Mix together the soy sauce, sugar and sesame oil. Set aside.

Put a wok or a large cast-iron frying pan to heat over a medium-high flame. When hot, put in the peanut oil. It should heat up in seconds. Now put in the garlic. Stir once or twice. Put in the red pepper. Stir once and put in the drained green beans. Stir them around until a few are lightly scorched. Pour in the soy sauce mixture. Continue to stir and fry until most of the sauce is absorbed. Turn the heat down and taste for salt: you might want to add a little bit more. Stir to mix and serve.

YELLOW RICE WITH CARROTS, RAISINS AND SESAME SEEDS
Serves 6

Long-grain rice (if you can find basmati, do use it), measured to the 15-fl oz/425-ml/2 cup level in a glass measuring jug
2 tablespoons/30ml vegetable oil
A 1-in/2.5-cm stick cinnamon
¼ teaspoon celery seeds
2 teaspoons/10ml sesame seeds
1 tablespoon/15ml golden raisins/sultanas
1 medium-sized carrot, peeled and coarsely grated
¼ teaspoon ground turmeric
1 teaspoon/5ml salt

Wash the rice in several changes of water. Drain. Cover well with water and leave to soak for 30 minutes. Drain thoroughly.

Heat the oil in a heavy pot over a medium flame. When hot, put in the cinnamon and celery seeds. Stir once and put in the sesame seeds. Stir once and put in the raisins. Stir once and quickly put in the drained rice, carrots, turmeric and salt. Sauté the rice for 1–2 minutes or until it turns translucent, turning the heat down a bit if it sticks. Now add 1 pint/ 570ml/2⅔ cups water and bring to a boil. Cover tightly, turn heat to very low, and cook for 25 minutes. Turn off heat and let pot sit, covered, for 5 minutes. Mix gently and remove the cinnamon stick before serving.

We love this rice. Every last grain is scraped out of the pot and devoured.

Overleaf
TOP: TASTY GREEN BEANS WITH SOY SAUCE DRESSING AND YELLOW RICE WITH CARROTS, RAISINS AND SESAME SEEDS. CENTRE: HOT SWEET AND SOUR PEANUT SAUCE. BOTTOM: GRILLED (BROILED) CORIANDER-HONEY CHICKEN

WHEN FRESH DILL IS IN SEASON

CHICKEN WITH FRESH DILL
DOUBLE PEPPER BROCCOLI
RICE FLAVOURED WITH CHICKEN BROTH AND VERMOUTH

'Will Ilena be here in time for dinner?'

'Probably,' says my youngest daughter, Sakina.

'Do you think Julie will stay to eat with us?'

'I don't know. I'll ask her when she comes,' says my eldest daughter, Zia.

I do not know about your children, but I can never pin mine down. They and their friends come and go at will, all driven by their own youthful, unpredictable clocks.

It is my task to prepare the meal. So, if I'm expecting an uncertain number of young people, I usually play it safe and make plenty of food. Chicken is easy to cook. It can also be so refreshing and elegant when simmered with fresh dill, yoghurt and lemon. (Leftovers are excellent the next day, hot or cold.)

The double pepper broccoli is stir-fried quickly with both sweet and hot red peppers, giving the meal a lovely accent. If you have never cooked rice with herbs and vermouth, you do not know what you are missing. We all love it and it is just right for soaking up all the delicious chicken juices. This meal can be put together very easily and quickly.

CHICKEN WITH FRESH DILL

Serves 8

I often make this dish in the country for dinner if friends are visiting or our daughters have arrived with their boyfriends. It can even be cooked ahead of time and then reheated.

Since hot green chillies vary in their fieriness, use as many as discretion permits. If you do not like hot food, leave them out altogether.

15fl oz/425ml/2 cups plain yoghurt
2 loosley packed teacups of finely chopped fresh dill
4 spring onions (scallions), cut into fine rings all the way up their green sections
1 tablespoon/15ml very finely grated, peeled fresh ginger
1½ tablespoons/22.5ml ground cumin seeds
1–6 fresh hot green chillies, very finely chopped
3 tablespoons/45ml lemon juice
6½lb/3kg chicken parts (I use just legs and breasts)
Salt
Freshly ground black pepper
5 tablespoons/75ml vegetable oil
A 1-in/2.5-cm stick of cinnamon
6 whole cloves

Put the yoghurt in a bowl and beat lightly with a fork or whisk until light and creamy. Add the dill, spring onions (scallions), ginger, cumin, green chillies, lemon juice, ½ teaspoon/2.5ml salt and some freshly ground black pepper. Mix well and set aside.

Skin the chicken pieces, dividing each leg into 2 and each breast into 4 sections. Sprinkle the chicken pieces on both sides with about 2 teaspoons/10ml salt and some black pepper.

Heat the oil in a wide non-stick pot over a medium-high flame. When hot, put in the cinnamon and cloves. Stir once and then put in as many chicken pieces as the pot will hold in a single layer. Brown on both sides. Remove to a bowl. Do all the chicken this way.

Put the chicken and all accumulated juices back in the pot. Put in the yoghurt and the dill. Mix and bring to a boil. Cover, turn heat to low and simmer about 20 minutes or until chicken is just tender. Stir gently two or three times during this period. (This dish can be cooked ahead up to this point.) Remove cover, turn heat up a bit, and boil away a lot of the liquid, stirring the chicken gently every now and then. A thick sauce should just cling to the chicken pieces.

DOUBLE PEPPER BROCCOLI

Serves 6–8

This dish has two kinds of red pepper – the fresh sweet variety and the dried, fiery kind. However, this is not a hot dish. Because the hot peppers are stir-fried rather quickly, all they do is lend the flavour and aroma of their skins to the dish but none of their heat. I use olive oil for the cooking. It might seem a bit unusual, but you will see how good it is.

1 large head (2½lb/1125g) broccoli
1 whole fresh sweet red pepper
5 tablespoons/75ml olive oil
1 tablespoon/15ml whole yellow mustard seeds
2 whole dried hot red peppers
¾–1 teaspoon/4–5ml salt
3 tablespoons/45ml chicken broth or stock (home-made or canned) or water

Cut the broccoli into delicate florets, peeling the slim stalks where necessary. Peel all the coarser stalks and then cut them into ½-in/1.5-cm thick rounds.

Cut the sweet red pepper lengthwise into ⅛-in/3-mm wide strips, removing the seeds as you go.

Heat the oil in a wok over a high flame. When hot, put in the mustard seeds. As soon as they begin to pop, put in the dried red peppers. Stir once and put in the broccoli. Stir a few times until the broccoli is bright green. Add the sweet red pepper and salt. Stir once or twice. Add the stock, cover and turn heat to medium-low. Cook 3–4 minutes or until the broccoli is crisp-tender. Remove the cover, raise the heat a bit, and boil away any liquid.

RICE FLAVOURED WITH CHICKEN BROTH AND VERMOUTH

Serves 6–8

I have been making this rice dish for the last twenty years. Our kids, rather simply, refer to it as 'chicken broth rice'. You can throw into it any herbs that you happen to have – parsley, thyme, summer savory – even mixtures such as 'Provençal herbs' are good.

Long-grain rice, measured to the 1¼-pint/720-ml/3 cup level in a glass measuring jug
3 tablespoons/45ml vegetable oil
1 small onion, peeled and thinly sliced into half-rings
1 teaspoon/5ml dried Provençal herbs, or ½ teaspoon dried thyme (see note above)
28fl oz/775ml/3½ cups chicken broth or stock (canned or freshly made)
4fl oz/120ml/½ cup dry vermouth
Salt

Wash the rice in several changes of water. Cover with fresh water and leave to soak for 30 minutes. Drain.

Heat the oil in a heavy-bottomed pot over medium-high heat. When hot, put in the onion. Stir and fry until lightly browned. Put in the herbs and stir once. Add the drained rice and stir. Lower the heat to medium. Stir and sauté the rice for 2–3 minutes until translucent. Add the chicken broth, vermouth and about 2 teaspoons/10ml salt if the broth is unsalted, less if it is. Bring to a boil. Cover tightly, turn the heat to very low and cook for 25 minutes.

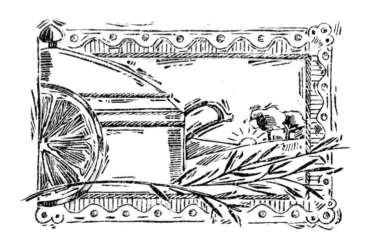

WHEN FRUIT LENDS A HAND

ROAST CHICKENS STUFFED WITH SPICED APPLES
RICE WITH ORANGE RIND AND SPRING ONIONS (SCALLIONS)
KALE OR SPRING GREENS (COLLARD GREENS)
COOKED IN BROTH

In upstate New York, we are surrounded by apple trees that begin to produce vigorously in the later part of the summer. We eat some of the fruit out of hand and some we make into pies and sauces. A great many of the hardier apples we wrap in newspapers and store in our cool, airy larder to use through the winter.

Among the dishes that I make with the apples is this simple roast chicken. The spicy apple stuffing gives the chicken a most pleasing sweet and sour quality. The fruitiness of the meal is further accented by the orange rind in the rice. Then, to give the menu a surprising twist, I cook the kale with hot chillies – not too many, mind you, just enough to provide a needed contrast to the flavours of the fruit.

ROAST CHICKENS STUFFED WITH SPICED APPLES

Serves 6

Here is an absolutely delightful dish, combining hot, sweet, sour and salty flavours – all at their gentlest and mildest. I prefer to use two smaller chickens rather than one large one as they cook much faster.

For the Chickens

2 chickens, each 3½–4 lb/1.25–1.35kg
2 tablespoons/30ml olive oil
½ teaspoon/2.5ml paprika
Salt
Freshly ground black pepper
¼ teaspoon dried thyme
¼ teaspoon cayenne pepper

For the Stuffing

4 medium-sized hard, tart apples
3 tablespoons/45ml lemon juice
½ teaspoon/2.5ml salt
Freshly ground black pepper
2½ tablespoons/37ml sugar
¼ teaspoon cayenne pepper
¼ teaspoon dried thyme
¼ teaspoon ground cinnamon

Remove the innards from the chickens (save for a soup). Pat the chickens dry. Mix oil and paprika in a small bowl and brush on to chickens. Dust chickens with salt, lots of black pepper, thyme and cayenne pepper. Set aside.

Preheat oven to 450°F/230°C/Gas Mark 8.

Peel the apples, core them and chop them into ¼in/6mm dice. Put in a bowl. Add all the other ingredients for stuffing and toss. Stuff inside the chickens. Close the chicken cavities by overlapping the skin and sticking toothpicks in it. Place chickens on a rack set over a baking pan and bake for 20 minutes. Turn heat to 325°F/170°C/Gas Mark 3 and bake for another 40–50 minutes or until the legs move easily in their sockets. Baste a few times with the pan juices while baking. Let the chickens rest for 15 minutes before carving. Remove toothpicks. Serve each person some of the stuffing along with their portion of chicken.

RICE WITH ORANGE RIND AND SPRING ONIONS (SCALLIONS)

Serves 6

You will love this rice. It has the marmalade-like pungency of orange rind, the sweetness of sultanas (raisins) and the savoury earthiness of the rice. I use packaged American long-grain rice here and do not even bother to wash or soak it.

The rind from a quarter of an orange (make sure you have none of the white pith), cut off in long strips
3 tablespoons/45ml vegetable oil
Long-grain rice, measured to the 15-fl oz/ 425-ml/2 cup level in a glass measuring jug
⅛ teaspoon ground turmeric
2 spring onions (scallions), cut all the way up their green sections into thin rounds
2 tablespoons/30ml sultanas (golden raisins)
2 teaspoons/10ml sugar
1 teaspoon/5ml salt
¼ teaspoon ground allspice

Cut the orange rind into very fine matchsticks about 1½in/4cm long. Drop into a small pot of boiling water. Boil for 30 seconds and then drain. Leave in the strainer.

Heat the oil in a heavy-bottomed medium-sized pot over a medium flame. When hot, put in the rice, rind, turmeric, spring onions (scallions), sultanas (raisins), sugar, salt and allspice. Stir and sauté for a minute or two or until the rice turns translucent, lowering the heat a bit if it sticks. Now put in 1¼ pints/ 700ml/3 cups water and bring to a boil. Cover tightly, turn the heat to very low and cook for 25 minutes.

KALE OR SPRING GREENS (COLLARD GREENS) COOKED IN BROTH

Serves 6

This method of cooking these greens is Kashmiri in inspiration, though I have made some changes such as using olive oil instead of mustard oil and using broth instead of water. These greens can easily be cooked ahead of time and refrigerated for two days.

4 lb/1.75kg kale or spring greens (collard greens)
1½ pints/845ml/4 cups chicken broth or stock, canned or home-made
4 cloves garlic, peeled
1–2 fresh hot green chillies, whole
1–2 dried hot red peppers
3 tablespoons/45ml olive oil
Salt to taste

Trim greens, discarding the tough lower stems. Wash well. Cut the leafy sections into 1-in/ 2.5-cm wide strips.

In a large pot, combine the broth, garlic, green chillies, red peppers and olive oil. Bring to a boil. Add the greens and cover. Reduce heat a bit and cook until the greens wilt, stirring once or twice during this period. Turn the heat to low and simmer for 20–45 minutes or until the greens are tender. Remove the cover, turn the heat to high and cook rapidly until most of the liquid evaporates.

If you like, remove the whole chillies before serving.

SHADES OF OLD PERSIA

CHICKEN LEGS COOKED WITH FRESH GREEN CORIANDER
(CHINESE PARSLEY) AND SULTANAS (GOLDEN RAISINS)
GREEN BEANS WITH MUSHROOMS AND POTATOES
CAULIFLOWER FLAVOURED WITH THYME
ONION RELISH WITH MINT
PITA BREAD

Stews – all manner of stews – may be made ahead of time and refrigerated. As the spices penetrate, the flavour intensifies.

This meal has two stews in it, each quite different from the other. The combination of fresh green coriander (Chinese parsley) and sultanas (golden raisins) in the chicken stew gives the meat a sprightly, sweet taste – assertive, but not at all overpowering. The green beans, on the other hand, are stewed with mushrooms, potatoes and tomatoes, each vegetable flavouring the other most helpfully. The onion relish may be made several hours in advance as well.

The only dish to be made at the last minute is the cauliflower, which I flavour with just a little thyme. I have the florets cut and ready. The stir-frying takes all of 5 minutes.

I sometimes serve store-bought pita bread on the side, though this is not necessary. To heat pita breads, wrap them in foil and then put them in a 400°F/200°C/Gas Mark 6 oven for 10–15 minutes.

CHICKEN LEGS COOKED WITH FRESH GREEN CORIANDER (CHINESE PARSLEY) AND SULTANAS (GOLDEN RAISINS)

Serves 6–8

This is a mild, Persian-style dish with a gentle mixture of sweet and sour flavours.

10 whole chicken legs, weighing about 6 lb/ 2.75kg, or 10 drumsticks and 10 thighs
6 tablespoons/90ml vegetable oil
A 2-in/5-cm stick cinnamon
6 whole cardamom pods
10 whole cloves
1 large onion, peeled and cut into fine half-rings
15fl oz/425ml/2 cups plain yoghurt, beaten lightly until smooth and creamy
1 lightly packed teacup chopped fresh green coriander (Chinese parsley)
2 tablespoons/30ml sultanas (golden raisins)
1 teaspoon/5ml ground cumin seeds
1 tablespoon/15ml ground coriander seeds
1½ teaspoons/7.5ml salt

Skin the chicken legs, and if whole, divide into drumsticks and thighs. If drumsticks and thighs are separated already, just skin them.

Heat the oil in a large, wide, preferably non-stick, pot over a high flame. When hot, put in the cinnamon, cardamom and cloves. Stir once and put in the onion. Stir and fry until the onion is medium brown in colour. Put in the chicken pieces. Stir and fry them for 6–8 minutes or until they pick up a few brown spots. Now put in all the remaining ingredients and bring to a boil. Turn the heat to low, cover and simmer gently for 20 minutes. Remove the cover, turn the heat up and boil away most of the thin sauce. You should have just a little very thick sauce left at the bottom of the pot.

NB The large whole spices are not meant to be eaten.

Previous page

CLOCKWISE FROM THE TOP: PITA BREAD, ONION RELISH WITH MINT, GREEN BEANS WITH MUSH-ROOMS AND POTATOES, CAULIFLOWER FLAVOURED WITH THYME, CHICKEN LEGS COOKED WITH FRESH GREEN CORIANDER (CHINESE PARSLEY) AND SULTANAS (GOLDEN RAISINS)

GREEN BEANS WITH MUSHROOMS AND POTATOES

Serves 6–8

In India, we often cook several vegetables together, thus minimizing the use of pots and pans – as well as saving on fuel. Each vegetable shares its flavours with the next to give the dish an added, delightful dimension.

A ½-in/1.5-cm cube of fresh ginger, peeled
4 tablespoons/60ml vegetable oil
1 teaspoon/5ml whole cumin seeds
1 medium-sized onion, peeled and cut into fine half-rings
3 medium-sized potatoes (1 lb/450g), peeled, cut into half lengthwise, and then cut crosswise into ½-in/1.5-cm thick segments
½lb/225g mushrooms, cut into thick slices
1½lb/675g green beans, trimmed and cut into 1-in/2.5-cm pieces
¼ teaspoon ground turmeric
½ teaspoon/2.5ml cayenne pepper
1 tablespoon/15ml ground coriander seeds
2 teaspoons/10ml salt

Cut the ginger into very thin slices. Stack the slices and cut them into very thin strips.

Heat the oil in a large frying pan or a large, wide pot over a medium-high flame. When hot, put in the cumin seeds. Let them sizzle for a few seconds. Now put in the ginger. Stir for a minute. Put in the onions. Stir and fry until the onion turns light brown. Put in the potatoes. Stir and fry them for 3-4 minutes. Add the mushrooms. Stir for a minute or so or until the mushrooms begin to glisten. Put in the beans, turmeric, cayenne, coriander and salt. Stir once or twice. Add 8fl oz/237ml water and bring to a boil. Cover, turn heat to low, and simmer for about 25–30 minutes or until all the vegetables are tender. There should be no thin liquid left. If there is any, just boil it away.

CAULIFLOWER FLAVOURED WITH THYME

Serves 4–6

Another very easy, very quick and very delicious dish. Just make sure that you cut the
cauliflower evenly into small, delicate bite-
sized florets, each with a head no wider than
1in/2.5cm and a stem no longer than 1½in/
4cm.

1 smallish head cauliflower (1¾lb/800g)
4 tablespoons/60ml vegetable oil
1 teaspoon/5ml whole yellow mustard seeds
¼ teaspoon dried thyme
½–¾ teaspoon/2.5–4ml salt
Freshly ground black pepper

Cut the cauliflower into small florets (see note
above).

Heat the oil in a large frying pan or a large
wok over a medium-high flame. When hot, put
in the mustard seeds. As soon as they begin to
pop (this takes just a few seconds), put in the
thyme. Stir once and put in the cauliflower. Stir
and fry the cauliflower for 2–3 minutes. Now
sprinkle in the salt. Add 4 tablespoons/60ml

water and cover immediately. Cook over the
same medium-high flame for about 2–4 minutes or until the cauliflower is just tender, but
retains a slight crunch. Uncover, and boil away
the extra liquid if there is any. Check for salt
and add some black pepper.

ONION RELISH WITH MINT

Serves 6–8

2 medium-sized onions, peeled
1¼ teaspoons/6.25ml salt – or to taste
About 2½ tablespoons/37ml lemon juice
⅛ teaspoon cayenne pepper
1 tablespoon/15ml finely chopped fresh mint

Cut the onions into paper-thin slices and put
them in a bowl. Add all the other seasonings.
Mix, separating the onion slices into rings as
you do so. Taste for seasoning, making adjust-
ments if necessary. Set aside for 30 minutes or
longer, for the flavours to blend.

COOKING WITH CHICKPEAS

SPICY CHICKEN STEWED WITH CHICKPEAS
STIR-FRIED GINGERY AUBERGINE (EGGPLANT)
GREEN BEANS WITH GARLIC AND CHERRY PEPPERS

The hearty chicken stew is piquantly spiced with ginger, green chillies and coriander seeds. It can conveniently be made well ahead of time and refrigerated. Its flavour improves as the hours pass.

I serve it with two vegetables – stir-fried aubergine (eggplant) which may be made ahead of time and reheated, and crunchy garlicky beans, which should be finished off at the last minute. Store-bought French or Italian bread, or even pita bread, may be served on the side.

SPICY CHICKEN STEWED WITH CHICKPEAS

Serves 4–6

Here is a substantial, nutritious stew, just perfect for a cool night. This recipe calls for canned chickpeas. If you wish to use the dried variety, soak 6oz/180g/¾ cup dry chickpeas overnight in water. Drain. Boil in 2 pints/1.14 litres/5 cups fresh water for 1–3 hours or until tender. Add about ¾ teaspoon/4ml salt in the last 15 minutes of cooking. Drain and use. The liquid from the chickpeas may be used for cooking the stew.

8–10 cloves garlic, peeled
3 1-in/2.5-cm cubes of fresh ginger, peeled and coarsely chopped
2 fresh hot green chillies, chopped (optional)
3½lb/1.5kg chicken, cut up into serving pieces
Salt
Freshly ground black pepper
3 tablespoons/45ml vegetable oil
2 tablespoons/30ml ground coriander seeds
1 tablespoon/15ml ground cumin seeds
½ teaspoon/2.5ml cayenne pepper
8–10 canned Italian plum tomatoes, chopped
A 19-oz/500g can of cooked chickpeas, drained (see note above for raw chickpeas)

Put the ginger, garlic, green chillies and 6 tablespoons/90ml water into the container of an electric blender. Blend until smooth.

Dust the chicken lightly on both sides with salt and pepper. Heat the oil in a large wide pot over a medium-high flame. Brown the chicken pieces, a few at a time, on both sides. Remove with tongs and keep in a bowl. When all the chicken is done, put the garlic-ginger paste into the same pot, turning the heat to medium as you do so. Fry the paste for 2 minutes, scraping up all the pan juices. Add the coriander, cumin and cayenne. Stir once or twice. Add the tomatoes. Stir and fry for another 2 minutes. Now put in the chicken and ¾ pint/425ml/2 cups water. Add about 1 teaspoon/5ml salt and bring to a boil. Cover, turn heat to low, and simmer for 20 minutes. Add the chickpeas. Simmer for another 10 minutes. Remove the cover, raise the flame a bit, and boil away any thin liquid: only a thick sauce should be left.

STIR-FRIED GINGERY AUBERGINE (EGGPLANT)

Serves 4–6

I make this with the slim, long pinkish-mauve aubergines (eggplants). If you cannot find them, use the ordinary kind, cut into 1-in/2.5-cm dice.

1½lb/675g aubergines (eggplants)
Salt
A 1-in/2.5-cm cube of fresh ginger, peeled and cut into minute dice
6 tablespoons/90ml vegetable oil
½ teaspoon/2.5ml whole cumin seeds
2 whole dried hot red peppers
1 tablespoon/15ml or more lemon juice
6 tablespoons/90ml chicken broth or stock, home-made or canned
Freshly ground black pepper

Cut the aubergines (eggplants) crosswise into 1-in/2.5-cm chunks. Put in a bowl. Sprinkle with ¾ teaspoon/4ml salt and rub it in. Set aside for one hour. Drain, and very gently squeeze out as much moisture as possible. Pat dry.

Heat the oil in a wok or large frying pan over a high flame. When hot, put in the cumin seeds. Five seconds later, put in the red peppers. Stir once, and put in the ginger. Stir once or twice and put in the aubergine (eggplant) pieces. Stir for a minute or two. Put in the lemon juice and broth. Cover immediately and turn heat to low. Simmer for 8–10 minutes or until the aubergine (eggplant) is just tender. Stir gently once or twice during this cooking period, replacing the cover each time. Check for salt and sourness. Sprinkle with ground pepper and toss gently.

GREEN BEANS WITH GARLIC AND CHERRY PEPPERS

Serves 4–6

An easy and wonderful way to cook green beans.

1½lb/675g green beans
Salt
4 tablespoons/60ml olive oil
2 cloves garlic, peeled and very finely chopped
1 pickled hot cherry pepper, cut into 8 sections, or any pickled pepper, coarsely sliced
Freshly ground black pepper
1 tablespoon/15ml finely choppped fresh parsley

Trim the ends of the green beans, but otherwise leave them whole. Bring a large pot of water to a rolling boil. Put in 1 tablespoon/15ml salt and stir. Now put in the beans and boil rapidly for 3–4 minutes or until they are crisp-tender. Drain.

Heat the oil in a large wide pot or a large frying pan over a high flame. When hot, put in the garlic. Stir once or twice or until the garlic browns lightly. Put in the beans and turn the heat down to medium. Toss the beans around in the oil for 30 seconds. Put in the cherry pepper and give another stir or two. Add a little more salt if you think you need it. Grind in some black pepper, add the parsley and toss again. Serve.

Overleaf
CLOCKWISE FROM THE TOP: BROCCOLI WITH CHERRY TOMATOES, SPECIAL SAN ANTONIO SALSA, CASSEROLE OF FRAGRANT CHICKEN AND RICE

A COSY MEAL

CASSEROLE OF FRAGRANT CHICKEN AND RICE
SPECIAL SAN ANTONIO SALSA
BROCCOLI WITH CHERRY TOMATOES
COLD BEER

With a good pilaf – a casserole of rice and chicken in this case – not much else is needed. Perhaps a salad and a good red wine, or else a crunchy green vegetable, a spicy relish and some beer. This makes for a cosy, homely meal, the kind a restaurant rarely supplies. I often make it for my family and dear friends. It requires no great strain and leaves everyone feeling quite comforted.

The *salsa* is served on the side, as you would a hot chutney. Take just small amounts of it, as it can be fiery!

CASSEROLE OF FRAGRANT CHICKEN AND RICE

Serves 4

It is believed that rice originated in Asia – whether it was in India, northern Thailand or Southern China, all of which vie for the honour, is hard to say.

All Asians love their rice. At times they eat it plain, relishing its pure taste and soothing texture, but they have over the centuries also learned to combine it with various vegetables, legumes, fish, poultry and meat to make what might be called casseroles – one-meal dishes. The grandest of these, to my mind, are the pilafs.

This pilaf here is a combination of what I've eaten in Mexico and the Philippines with some Indian know-how thrown in. It is simple to make – it does indeed require just one pot – and so deliciously satisfying as well.

4 whole chicken legs or 4 chicken drumsticks and 4 chicken thighs weighing about 1¾lb/ 800g in all
Salt
1 teaspoon/5ml dried oregano
Freshly ground black pepper
2 tablespoons/30ml lemon juice
Long-grain rice, measured to the 1¼ pint/ 720ml/3 cup level in a glass measuring jug
4 tablespoons/60ml vegetable oil
1 good-sized onion (5oz/140g), peeled, and cut into very fine half-rings
2 large cloves garlic, peeled and very finely chopped
1 teaspoon/5ml peeled and very finely grated fresh ginger
½ teaspoon/2.5ml paprika
1¾ pints/1 litre/4 cups chicken broth or stock, home-made or canned

If you have whole chicken legs, separate the drumsticks from the thighs. Skin all the chicken pieces. Cut deep diagonal slashes, 2 on each side of the drumsticks going all the way to the bone. Cut 2 diagonal slashes on the meaty side of each thigh, making sure you do not go right to an edge. Lay the chicken pieces out in a single layer on a large plate. Sprinkle with ¼ teaspoon salt, half the oregano, lots of black pepper and 1 tablespoon/15ml lemon juice. Rub the seasonings in. Turn the chicken pieces over, sprinkling with another ¼ teaspoon salt, the remaining oregano, more black pepper and the remaining lemon juice, rubbing these in as well. Set aside for 30 minutes or so.

Wash the rice in several changes of water. Drain. Cover well with fresh water and leave to soak for 30 minutes. Drain.

Heat the oil in a large wide pot over a medium-high flame. When hot, put in the onion. Stir and fry the onion until it turns medium brown. Put in the garlic and stir once or twice. Put in the ginger and stir once. Now put in the chicken. Stir and fry for 4–5 minutes. Turn heat down a bit and put in the paprika. Stir for another 30 seconds. Now put in the drained rice. Stir and sauté the rice for 2–3 minutes, gently scraping up anything that may have stuck to the bottom of the pan. Add the chicken broth and any liquid that may have accumulated on the chicken plate as well as 1 teaspoon/5ml salt (more if the stock is un-salted). Bring to a boil. Cover tightly, first with foil, crimping the edges, and then with a lid. Turn the heat to very low and cook for 35 minutes.

SPECIAL SAN ANTONIO SALSA

Serves 4–6

This sauce is an all-purpose dip which I have eaten only once, in a San Antonio, Texas, restaurant. It differs from other Mexican-style *salsas* in that the tomatoes and green chillies are roasted before they are blended, giving this sauce a rather dark look. You may make it as hot as you like. I have used 3 *jalapeño* peppers in this recipe which makes it very hot. You could use more or less, as you like.

2 medium-sized (10oz/285g in all) ripe tomatoes
3 *jalapeño* peppers or 6 fresh hot green chillies
¾ teaspoon/4ml salt

Hold the tomatoes one at a time over an open flame with tongs, and roast on all sides until they are blackened. Chop coarsely and put in a blender container. Roast the hot peppers over an open flame in the same way until blackened. Put into the same blender. Add the salt and blend until smooth.

BROCCOLI WITH CHERRY TOMATOES
Serves 4

This dish is best made in a wok, though a large frying pan will do.

1 medium-sized head of purple heating broccoli or 1½–2lb green broccoli
3 tablespoons/45ml olive or other vegetable oil
½ teaspoon/2.5ml whole cumin seeds
1 large clove garlic, peeled and very finely chopped
A quarter of a medium-sized onion, peeled and chopped
Salt
4 tablespoons/60ml chicken broth or stock (home-made or canned)
½lb/225g cherry tomatoes, halved

Cut the broccoli into florets (reserve the stems for another dish – or for eating raw). You should have about 1 lb/450g florets.

Heat the oil in a wok or large frying pan over a medium-high flame. When hot, put in the cumin seeds. A few seconds later, put in the garlic and onion. Stir for a few seconds. Put in the broccoli and salt. Stir until the broccoli turns bright green. Put in the chicken broth. Cover, turn the heat to medium, and cook for 2–3 minutes or until the broccoli is done but retains some crispness. While it is cooking, salt the tomato halves lightly. Uncover the wok or frying pan, raise the heat again to dry out the liquid, and add the tomatoes. Stir for 30 seconds and serve.

AFTER-THE-THEATRE SUPPER

CHAWANMUSHI (LIGHT CUSTARD-SOUP) WITH PRAWNS
(SHRIMP) AND WATERCRESS
ORANGE-FLAVOURED STIR-FRIED CHICKEN
SALAD OF GREENS AND PEPPERS

How many times have you gone to the theatre and then searched around desperately for a decent place to eat a late supper? Most places of any worth invariably close their doors at times that, understandably, suit their master-chefs. I find it easier to bring people home where we can all drink and eat at leisure.

Sometimes I offer guests a full dinner – especially if it is a Friday or Saturday. But on weekdays I make what can be described as a 'light repast' – meals such as this one.

The first course here is a savoury custard that is so light that in Japan, where it originated (all right, the Japanese got it from the Chinese), it is served as a soup. I serve the second course, a Chinese stir-fry dish, on a bed of shredded and dressed salad greens.

If I have time during the day, I make a strawberry tart. When I am rushed, I either buy dessert or serve coffee and tea with the most elegant biscuits or cookies from our local bakery.

This menu can be organized so that all the chopping and cutting is done ahead of time. You should do only a minimum amount when your guests are with you. I usually pour myself a drink and take a friend or two into the kitchen as I finish off the dishes

AFTER-THE-THEATRE SUPPER IN STAGES

Here is how you can prepare the meal, doing most of the work before you go out:

1 Cut the chicken and put it in its first marinade for 30 minutes. Do the 'velveting' in water (see recipe). Cool and cover. Refrigerate only if it is a hot day.

2 Cut the orange strips and blanch them. Cut the spring onions (scallions), put on a small plate and cover with cling film (plastic wrap). Put the red peppers in a small bowl.

3 Mix the sauce ingredients for the chicken. Cover and refrigerate if it is a hot day.

4 Wash and cut all ingredients for salad. Cover and refrigerate. Make salad dressing and set aside.

5 Mix the egg-chicken stock mixture for the *chawanmushi*. Cover and refrigerate.

6 Marinate the prawns (shrimp). Prepare the water chestnuts and watercress. Cover and set aside.

7 Set up the wok on one burner. Find six 8-oz/237ml custard cups and see if they will fit easily in your steaming gadget. If you are using a roasting pan, set a trivet on the bottom. Check to see if the pan will fit on two burners, considering you also have a wok on the cooker. (Remember, you can always use the oven, but it will take longer.) Pour enough water into the steaming gadget so that it will come three-quarters of the way up the sides of the cups when you put them in.

8 Set your table.

Now go and enjoy the theatre.

9 When you return, offer your guests a drink, pour yourself one and take everything you need out of the refrigerator. Set the water boiling for the *chawanmushi*. Put the solids in the custard cups. Pour in the egg-chicken stock mixture through a strainer. Arrange the watercress leaves on top. Cover, and put the *chawanmushi* cups inside the simmering water to cook. Just before it is ready (remember, it takes 13 minutes), toss the salad and set it out on six plates.

10 Serve the guests the hot *chawanmushi*. Sit down and eat it yourself.

11 Come back into the kitchen to stir-fry the chicken. Put it on top of the salad and serve.

CHAWANMUSHI (LIGHT CUSTARD-SOUP) WITH PRAWNS (SHRIMP) AND WATERCRESS

Serves 6

Chawanmushi looks like an egg custard, but it is actually a barely set, savoury soup. It is eaten with a soup spoon. In Japan, it is cooked and served in a special cup which is rather like an 8-oz/237-ml egg coddler with a lid. You can improvise with small custard cups, ramekins, crème-brûlée cups, even small bowls.

You need a flat-surfaced steamer. Bamboo steamers are generally too small to hold six cups. Unless you have a large professional steamer, it is best to improvise: as I have said, I use a large roasting pan with its own trivet. The water in the pan should come three-quarters of the way up the sides of the custard cups and should be kept at a bare simmer. Always have extra hot water at the ready in a bubbling kettle in case you run out of it. (Alternatively, the covered steaming pot can go into an oven preheated to 425°F/220°C/Gas Mark 7 for 30 minutes.)

If you remember that for every large egg you need about 5fl oz/150ml of liquid, you can easily increase or decrease this recipe.

6 small prawns (shrimp), peeled and deveined
2 teaspoons/10ml plus 1 tablespoon/15ml saké (Japanese rice wine)
A pinch plus a teaspoon/5ml sugar
½ teaspoon/2.5ml plus about 1 tablespoon/ about 15ml soy sauce
3 fresh water chestnuts, peeled and sliced, or 3 canned ones, removed from their liquid and sliced
6 small sprigs watercress
6 large eggs
1½ pints/845ml/3⅔ cups canned chicken broth or home-made stock

Wash the prawns (shrimp) well and pat them dry. Put in a bowl. Add 2 teaspoons/10ml saké, a pinch of sugar, and ½ teaspoon/2.5ml soy sauce. Cover and refrigerate.

Put the water chestnuts and watercress on separate plates. Cover and set aside.

Beat the eggs lightly (*not* to a froth) in a

bowl. Add the chicken broth, 1 tablespoon/ 15ml saké, 1 teaspoon/5ml sugar, and any-where from 1 teaspoon/5ml to 1 tablespoon/ 15ml soy sauce depending upon the saltiness of the broth. Mix. Cover and refrigerate.

About 20 minutes before eating, bring the water in the steamer to a simmer. Meanwhile, remove the prawns (shrimp) from their marinade. Put one prawn (shrimp) and a couple of slices of water chestnut into each custard cup. Strain the egg-chicken broth mixture over the prawns (shrimp), dividing it evenly amongst the 6 cups. Float the watercress pieces over the top. Cover the custard cups with lids or with foil, and lower into the simmering water. Cover the steaming pot and simmer very very gently – the water should hardly bubble – for 13 minutes. Remove and serve hot.

ORANGE-FLAVOURED STIR-FRIED CHICKEN

Serves 6

Chicken pieces, especially breast meat, stay much more tender if they are 'velveted' – that is, passed through barely simmering water, before they are stir-fried. I serve this dish over a bed of fresh greens, but you could if you like serve it all by itself.

2 lb/900g boned and skinned chicken breasts
2 tablespoons/30ml dry sherry
2 tablespoons/30ml soy sauce
1 tablespoon/15ml oriental sesame oil
½ teaspoon/2.5ml peeled and finely grated fresh ginger
1 tablespoon/15ml cornflour (cornstarch)

Overleaf
CLOCKWISE FROM THE TOP: ORANGE-FLAVOURED STIR-FRIED CHICKEN, SALAD OF GREENS AND PEPPERS, CHAWANMUSHI (LIGHT CUSTARD SOUP) WITH PRAWNS (SHRIMP) AND WATERCRESS

For the Sauce

1½ teaspoons/7.5ml cornflour (cornstarch)
3 tablespoons/45ml soy sauce
1 teaspoon/5ml peeled and finely grated fresh ginger
2 teaspoons/10ml dry sherry
1 tablespoon/15ml oriental sesame oil
4 tablespoons/60ml chicken stock or water, home-made or canned
2 tablespoons/30ml orange juice
Freshly ground black pepper

You Also Need

Long strips of orange rind (without the white pith) cut off from a third of an orange
2 tablespoons/30ml vegetable oil
8–10 dried hot red peppers
4 spring onions (scallions), cut all the way up their green sections into thin rounds

Cut the chicken breasts into ¾-in/2-cm dice. Put in a bowl. Add the next five ingredients and mix well. Cover and set aside, refrigerating if necessary, for 30 minutes.

Mix all the ingredients for the sauce.

Cut the orange rind into matchsticks about 1½in/4cm long. Drop them into a small pot of boiling water and boil rapidly for 5 minutes. Drain.

Heat about 3¾ pints/2 litres/2qt of water in a wok over medium heat. When it is bubbling put in all the chicken. Turn the heat to medium low. Stir the chicken around until the pieces turn white all the way through. Drain. Cover and set aside. Do not refrigerate unless necessary.

Just before serving heat the 2 tablespoons/30ml vegetable oil over a high flame in a wok. When hot, put in the red peppers. Stir once or twice and put in the orange rind. Stir once and put in the spring onions (scallions). Stir once and turn the heat down a bit. Give the sauce a good stir and pour it into the wok. Stir a few times until it starts to thicken. Put in the chicken. Stir and fry for a few seconds until the chicken is warmed through and glistening with the sauce. Serve at once.

SALAD OF GREENS AND PEPPERS
Serves 6

I use this salad as a 'nest' for the preceding chicken dish. It adds freshness, crunch and vitamins. You can use almost any greens you like. They should be cut or torn into fairly fine shreds. A combination of cos (romaine), radicchio (if you can find or grow it), chicory (Belgian endive), and slivered red and green peppers is rather nice.

The dressing for this salad is oriental in nature. Use as much or as little as will just wet the greens.

The Dressing

2 tablespoons/30ml vinegar
2 teaspoons/10ml oriental sesame oil
2 tablespoons/30ml peanut or groundnut oil
1½ teaspoons/7.5ml soy sauce
¼ teaspoon salt
¼ teaspoon sugar

The Greens

A head of cos (romaine) lettuce
About half a head of radicchio
A third of a sweet red pepper, cut into fine slivers
A third of a sweet green pepper, cut into fine slivers
A few chicory (Belgian endive) leaves, cut into fine slivers

Combine all ingredients for the dressing and mix well.

Tear or cut the cos (romaine) and radicchio into fine strips. Add the red pepper, green pepper, chicory (Belgian endive), and mix. Just before serving, mix the dressing again, pour over the greens and toss.

A SPICY PICNIC

THAI-STYLE CHICKEN SALAD SERVED IN LETTUCE ROLLS
GREEN BEANS WITH TWO MUSTARDS
THE BEST, LIGHTEST POTATO SALAD
COLD LAGER
WATERMELON AND MANGO SLICES

We have a stream behind our country home. It is not exactly on *our* property. *We* can only boast of a bog. No, the stream runs through a series of our neighbour's fields that, over the years, we have come to know as well as our own land.

In midwinter, the stream is edged with a frothy frosting of soft snow and is criss-crossed by leaping, dancing deer. In the spring, it gushes forward with drunken speed, its wide waters an amalgam of melting ice and deep, hidden underwater reservoirs. It is hard to ford then, awesome and mighty as it thunders along. We stand on its shore, thanking the Lord for giving us a chance to live a mere stone's throw away. In the summer, the stream becomes gentle and accessible. The deer recede into the forested hills, three dozen cows (and a horse) start up their annual grazing routine on its banks, and *we* begin to carry to its shores first our drinks, and then our meals as well for impromptu picnics.

Picnics are good at all times, but spicy picnic foods are particularly good during the heat of midsummer, specially when accompanied by cold lager and followed by chilled watermelon and mango slices.

The Thai-style chicken salad, hot and tart, can be rolled up in lettuce leaves and nibbled while one cools one's feet in the stream. The green beans, left uncut, may be picked up with one's fingers and the potato salad, delicately spiced with cumin and spring onions (scallions) is just the perfect accompaniment.

For a picnic, all these foods can be packed in plastic containers, cooled in the refrigerator and then stacked inside insulated picnic baskets that have packs of dry ice in them.

THAI-STYLE CHICKEN SALAD SERVED IN LETTUCE ROLLS

Serves 4–6

There is a good reason why Steak Tartare – chopped and seasoned raw beef – has its name: it originated in central Asia and can still be found in many guises in parts of that continent. I ate a delicious version in northern Thailand. My hosts there had decided to scorch the beef slightly, but they let it remain quite raw inside. I have adapted their recipe to minced (ground) chicken breasts, cooking them through, but just barely. The dressing for the salad remains uniquely Thai, except that I have substituted soy sauce for the harder-to-find fish sauce.

In Thailand, this salad is served with a veritable forest of green herbs and raw vegetables, which are meant to be nibbled on the side. The 'forest' is designed and built up carefully so bits of red and orange (usually strips of peppers) peep through the dark and light green foliage (different types of lettuce, mint, green beans, etc). As the salad is tart and spicy, the raw vegetables act as a wonderful foil. I have used just lettuce and mint, but you can let your imagination run wild.

If you do not have shallots, use a 4-oz/115-g red onion. Peel it, cut it into very thin rounds and then quarter the rounds.

4 tablespoons/60ml long-grain rice
2 tablespoons/30ml vegetable oil
3 cloves garlic, peeled and finely chopped
2 boned and skinned chicken breasts (about 1¼lb/560g), minced (ground)
7 tablespoons/105ml lemon juice
4 tablespoons/60ml soy sauce
1 tablespoon/15ml sugar
½ teaspoon/2.5ml cayenne pepper
7 good-sized shallots (4oz/115g) peeled and cut into very fine slivers
4 tablespoons/60ml chopped fresh mint, as well as lots of mint sprigs

2 heads lettuce: 1 cos (romaine) and 1 cabbage (Boston) might be a good combination, the leaves separated, but left whole, washed and patted dry

Heat a small cast-iron frying pan over a medium flame. When hot, put in the rice. Stir and roast the rice until the grains are light brown (some grains will be darker, some lighter, some may even pop). Let cool slightly and then grind in a clean coffee grinder.

Heat the oil in a large wok over a high flame. When hot, put in the garlic. Stir once or twice or until the garlic turns light brown. Now put in the chicken, spreading it out in the wok. Let it brown very slightly in spots. Now, begin to stir it, breaking up the lumps as you do so. The chicken should just turn white and lose all its pinkness. Do not overcook. Remove from wok and put in a bowl.

Add the roasted and ground rice, lemon juice, soy sauce, sugar, cayenne pepper, shallots and chopped mint. Mix and taste for seasonings.

If you are eating in your own home, arrange the whole lettuce leaves and mint sprigs on one side of a very large platter. Put the chicken salad on the other side. To eat, spoon some of the salad on to the centre of a lettuce leaf, spreading it so it runs along the length. Put one or two sprigs of mint over the salad and then cover, first with one free end of the lettuce leaf and then the other, making a kind of roll.

For a picnic, pack the salad in one plastic container and all the greenery in another, much larger container. (Alternatively, roll all the lettuce leaves in a length of paper towel and put the whole thing inside a plastic bag. Empty the leaves into a bowl when serving.)

Previous Page
CLOCKWISE FROM THE TOP: WATERMELON AND MANGO SLICES, THE BEST, LIGHTEST POTATO SALAD, THAI-STYLE CHICKEN SALAD SERVED IN LETTUCE ROLLS, GREEN BEANS WITH TWO MUSTARDS

GREEN BEANS WITH TWO MUSTARDS
Serves 4–6

The pleasing, tangy taste of this salad is just perfect for balmy summer days.

Salt
3 tablespoons/45ml lemon juice
1 tablespoon/15ml Dijon-style mustard
Freshly ground black pepper
¼ teaspoon cayenne pepper
6 tablespoons/90ml olive oil
1½ tablespoons/22ml yellow mustard seeds
3 cloves garlic, peeled and cut into thin slivers
1½lb/675g green beans with their ends trimmed

Set a large pot of salted water to boil (the water should taste just a bit saltier than your natural preferences).

Put the lemon juice in a small bowl. Add the Dijon-style mustard, 1 teaspoon/5ml salt, black pepper and cayenne pepper. Mix.

Heat the oil in a small cast-iron frying pan over a medium flame. When hot, put in the mustard seeds. As soon as they start to pop (this just takes a few seconds), put in the garlic. Stir the garlic until the slivers turn light brown. Take the frying pan off the flame and let the oil cool just slightly. Beat the oil mixture into the lemon juice mixture until you have a creamy dressing.

The pot of water should now be at a rolling boil. Drop in the green beans. Boil vigorously for 3–5 minutes or until the beans are crisp-tender. Drain thoroughly. Put the beans into a large bowl. Beat the dressing once again and pour over the beans. Toss. Once the beans have cooled, they may be covered and refrigerated.

THE BEST, LIGHTEST POTATO SALAD
Serves 4–6

No mayonnaise is used here to bind the salad, just plain low-fat yoghurt. It is uncommonly good. The waxier the potatoes, the better the texture of the salad.

1¼lb/560g waxy boiling potatoes
8fl oz/237ml/1 cup plain, low-fat yoghurt
1 tablespoon/15ml vegetable oil
½ teaspoon/2.5ml whole cumin seeds
1 tablespoon/15ml whole yellow mustard seeds
¾ teaspoon/4ml salt
Freshly ground black pepper
1 spring onion (scallion) – just its white portion – cut into very, very fine rounds

Boil the potatoes in their jackets. Cool (do not refrigerate) and peel. Cut into ¾-in/2-cm dice.

Put the yoghurt in a bowl. Beat lightly with a fork until soft and creamy.

Heat the oil in a small frying pan. When hot, put in the cumin seeds. They should begin to sizzle within a few seconds. Put in the mustard seeds. As soon as they start to pop (a matter of seconds), empty all the contents of the frying pan – oil and spices – into the bowl with the yoghurt. Add salt, black pepper and spring onion (scallion). Stir to mix. Add the potatoes and mix gently. The potatoes may be refrigerated now if you so wish.

WATERMELON AND MANGO SLICES
Serves 4–6

Some people like to carry whole watermelons and mangoes to hilly picnic sites. We used to do that in India. Every summer, we vacationed in Himalayan mountain resorts, but our favourite mangoes were shipped to us, week after week, from the Plains where they grew. We would carry them in baskets to distant picnic sites and then immerse them in the cold, flowing waters of a stream. By the time we were ready to eat, they were all suitably chilled!

If your picnic site has no streams, I suggest you slice your fruit and put them in plastic containers, chilling them first in your refrigerator. The plastic containers can then be packed inside insulated picnic baskets.

Hard, semi-ripe mangoes can be ripened at home by wrapping them individually in newspaper, putting them in a basket or box and leaving them unrefrigerated for a few days – they should yield to the touch, but should not have black spots.

4 ripe, good-quality mangoes
½–1 watermelon, depending on size

Peel each mango and cut two thick slices off its flatter sides, leaving the stone in the middle. Now slice off the remaining flesh from the stone. (Do not just throw the mango stone away. Eat all the remaining flesh off it before you do so. This is your reward for all the trouble you are taking.) Put the mango slices in a plastic box and refrigerate until ready to be eaten or packed for the picnic.

Cut the watermelon into slices. Cut off the thick rinds and cut the flesh into chunks. Remove as many seeds as is easily possible. Put in a plastic box and refrigerate until ready to be eaten or packed for the picnic.

MAINLY MEAT

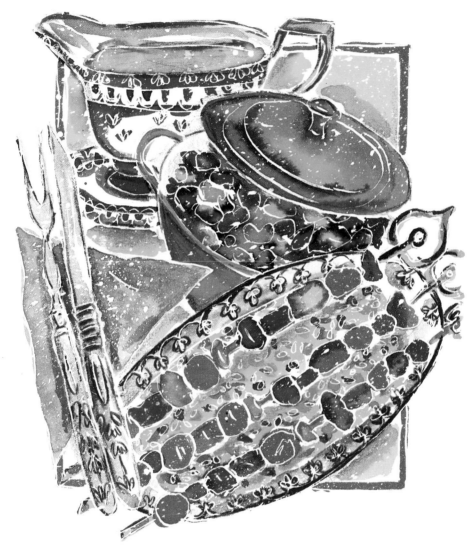

A FLAVOUR OF JAPAN

JAPANESE-STYLE CRAB AND CUCUMBER SALAD
SAKÉ
FIVE-MINUTE VEAL SCALLOPS COOKED IN
A JAPANESE STYLE
SPINACH FLAVOURED WITH HAM STRIPS AND SHALLOTS
LEMONY BROWN RICE

In Japan there are wonderful little salads and pickles and pickley salads that are served at the start of a meal with tiny cupfuls of warm saké. The salads, always small amounts, come in dainty individual bowls and plates, always mounded as if they were pretty hillocks. One stretches one's chopsticks toward them and picks up a nibblesworth. Then one sips the saké. It gives one a good feeling.

I often start meals with such a salad. It does not fill one up at all – just sends taste buds tingling. Here I combine cucumber with crab and put a hint of ginger in the dressing. You do not have to serve the saké if you do not want to: a white wine would be equally good. The salad may be made in advance and refrigerated.

The main dish in this meal, good for dinner or a late supper, consists of veal scallops which are sautéed quickly in a Japanese style with some mushrooms. They have the sprightly flavour of soy sauce and ginger and cook in just a few minutes. I leave them to the last. With the veal, I serve a brown rice that is very delicately seasoned with lemon rind. It can be cooked just before guests arrive and left in a warm place or, if you are serving a late after-the-theatre-supper, leave the rice soaking when you go out. You can add all the seasonings to the soaking water. Set it to cook the minute you come in. The rice will be ready by the time you finish your first course.

I also serve an Indonesian-style spinach which depends for its panache not only on the many shallots with which it is stir-fried, but – quite unusually – on slivers of ham. This spinach may be made ahead of time and reheated.

JAPANESE-STYLE CRAB AND CUCUMBER SALAD
Serves 4–6

A perky salad, its excellence depending much upon the sweetness of the crab. If you cannot find crab, poach a fillet of any flavourful white fish (such as red snapper, sea bass or pompano) or a salmon steak, flake it, and use that instead.

12oz/340g either pickling cucumbers (5 to 6) or English cucumbers
1 tablespoon/15ml salt
2 tablespoons/30ml distilled white vinegar
2 teaspoons/10ml sugar
2 teaspoons/10ml soy sauce
4 tablespoons/60ml chicken broth or stock, home-made or canned
½ teaspoon/2.5ml very finely grated, peeled fresh ginger
½lb/225g cooked lump crabmeat, fresh or canned, picked over for shell fragments

Scrub the cucumbers well and trim the ends. Peel, cut in half lengthwise and remove seeds. Cut crosswise into the thinnest possible slices. (A food processor does this job very fast.)

Put the salt and 4 cups water in bowl. Mix. Drop in the cucumber slices and leave for 30 minutes. Drain. Lift out a handful of cucumbers, cup them with the palm of your other hand and very gently squeeze out as much moisture as you can. Do this with all the cucumber.

Combine the vinegar, sugar, soy sauce, chicken broth and ginger. Taste for seasoning. Combine the cucumbers and the mixed seasonings in a bowl and toss. Leave for 5 minutes. Put in the crabmeat and toss again. Serve at room temperature or cold. (The Japanese like to mound up this salad in the centre of small individual bowls or plates.)

A NOTE ON SAKÉ

Saké, Japanese rice wine, may be drunk cool, poured straight from its cask or bottle, but its gentle aroma is sent swirling upwards when it has been warmed first. The Japanese start drinking their saké with salads and raw fish appetizers at the start of a meal and then continue to drink it as the meal progresses.

If you wish to serve hot saké, pour some of it into a bottle (the Japanese use very narrow-necked ceramic bottles, but clean glass ones will do) stand the bottle in a pot of water and heat the water over a low flame. The saké should be hot to the touch. (If you are particular about these things, about 130°F/54°C is a correct temperature to aim for.) Now pour a few sipfuls into small handle-less saké cups. If you do not have saké cups, use liqueur glasses of the smallest possible capacity. You are supposed to finish the cup – it *is* small – while the saké is still warm.

A saké bottle, rather like a bottle of wine, does not keep too well after it has been opened. Try and use it up within a few days. Saké that has been heated has had its aroma dispersed, so heat only as much as you need for one round. You can always do several batches.

FIVE-MINUTE VEAL SCALLOPS COOKED IN A JAPANESE STYLE
Serves 4

Very few main dishes cook faster than this one. It is gently flavoured and quite delicious.

4 tablespoons/60ml soy sauce
4 teaspoons/20ml sugar
2 teaspoons/10ml very finely grated peeled fresh ginger
6 tablespoons/90ml chicken broth or stock, home-made or canned
Salt
Freshly ground black pepper
4–5 tablespoons/60–75ml vegetable oil
8 veal scallops (about 1 lb/450g), pounded until they are ¼in/6mm thick
10 smallish mushrooms, quartered

Combine the soy sauce, sugar, ginger, chicken broth and some freshly ground black pepper. Mix and set aside. Lightly salt and pepper both sides of the veal scallops.

Heat 4 tablespoons/60ml oil in a large frying pan over a medium-high flame. When hot, put in as many veal scallops as the pan will hold easily in a single layer. Brown quickly, about 1–2 minutes on each side. As the scallops get done, lift them out with a slotted spatula and put in a warm place. Do all the scallops this way, adding more oil to the pan if necessary. Now put in the mushrooms and turn the heat to medium. Stir and fry the mushrooms for 30 seconds. Put in the soy sauce mixture. Stir, scraping up the pan juices, and cook rapidly for about a minute. Pour the sauce over the veal and serve immediately.

SPINACH FLAVOURED WITH HAM STRIPS AND SHALLOTS

Serves 4

An Indonesian friend cooked this for me in her open-to-the-sea-and-sky kitchen in Bali. She used pork meat but I have used ham instead: I like its slightly smoky flavour. There is actually very little ham in this dish – just enough to give it an added dimension and taste.

If you cannot find shallots, substitute thinly sliced red onion.

The hot red pepper lends both colour and sharpness. If you cannot find one, use green chillies for the heat, and slivers of sweet red pepper for their colour.

2 lb/900g fresh spinach, trimmed and washed
1 fresh hot red pepper – or to taste
2oz/60g thinly sliced boiled ham, cut into 1½-in/4-cm long matchsticks
Freshly ground black pepper
1 teaspoon/5ml plus 4 tablespoons/60ml/¼ cup vegetable oil
4oz/115g/½ cup shallots, peeled and slivered
Salt
1 teaspoon/5ml sugar

Previous Page
CLOCKWISE FROM THE TOP: LEMONY BROWN RICE, JAPANESE-STYLE CRAB AND CUCUMBER SALAD, FIVE-MINUTE VEAL SCALLOPS COOKED IN JAPANESE STYLE, SPINACH FAVOURED WITH HAM STRIPS AND SHALLOTS

Cut the spinach crosswise into 2-in/5-cm wide strips.

Cut the pepper lengthwise into thin, 1½-in/4-cm long strips.

Spread out the ham slivers. Dust them very lightly with black pepper. Rub 1 teaspoon/5ml oil on them.

Heat the 4 tablespoons/60ml/¼ cup oil in a large wok or wide, large pot over a medium-high flame. When hot, put in the slivers of ham. Stir and fry them until they are slightly brown. Put in the shallots. Stir and fry them for 2–3 minutes. Now put in the red pepper. Stir once or twice. Add the spinach, about ¾ teaspoon/4ml salt and the sugar, stirring to mix. Add 4fl oz/120ml/½ cup water, cover and cook on a medium-high flame for 5 minutes. Remove cover. Stir and mix.

LEMONY BROWN RICE

Serves 4

Long-grain brown rice, measured to the 12-fl oz/356-ml/1½ cup level in a glass measuring jug
1 teaspoon/5ml salt
1 tablespoon/15ml lemon juice
1 teaspoon/5ml finely grated lemon rind
1 bay leaf
2 tablespoons/30ml very finely chopped fresh parsley
2 tablespoons/30ml unsalted butter or olive oil

Wash the rice in several changes of water. Drain. Put in a bowl. Add 1¼pt/720ml/3 cups water and leave to soak for 1 hour or longer.

Put the rice and its soaking liquid in a small heavy pot. Add the salt, lemon juice, lemon rind, bay leaf and parsley. Bring to a boil. Cover tightly, turn the heat to very low and cook for 35 minutes. Turn the heat off and let the rice sit, covered and undisturbed, for another 10 minutes. Add the butter or oil and mix gently with a fork.

HINTS FROM A LONDON PUB

A KIND OF SHEPHERD'S PIE
A SPINACH AND LETTUCE SALAD WITH A LEMONY DRESSING
COLD LAGER

Whether you serve it for lunch or dinner or for a late after-the-theatre supper, as I often do, the pie here makes one of the world's best one-pot meals. I serve a salad as well just to add greenery and crunch. Nothing else is needed, except cold lager or a glass of red wine.

Instead of covering my shepherd's pie with mashed potato as is customary, I blanket it with overlapping slices of boiled potatoes. Underneath the potatoes is well-spiced lamb and underneath *that* some tomatoes and aubergine (eggplant). I cook all the elements that go into my pie dish well ahead of time. I assemble the pie and then cover and refrigerate it. I have my salad greens washed and the salad dressing sitting at the ready in the refrigerator. When my guests arrive – or we all return from the theatre together, as the case may be – all I have to do is pop the pie dish into the oven and then, at the appropriate moment, throw the dressing over my salad and toss it. By this time, I am *so* carefree, I can even whistle as I pour the drinks.

A Kind of Shepherd's Pie
Serves 4–6

An English actress – or, I should say, an aspiring English actress, as we were both students at London's Royal Academy of Dramatic Arts at the time – baked me my first shepherd's pie. It was almost thirty years ago. I had never eaten such a satisfying, soothing combination before – mashed potatoes on top and nicely seasoned minced (ground) meat on the bottom. Bridget McConnel, who is half English and half French, served it with a green salad, teaching me in one unforgettable day the wonders of a well-made shepherd's pie and – something much more basic – how to make a perfect vinaigrette.

For my version, which has strong Greek and Indian overtones, I must acknowledge another source as well. There is a bar in London's Hammersmith district, very close to the Lyric Theatre, that makes a mean shepherd's pie, heavily accented with thyme. I have demolished many of these pies – all nice and hot from the oven – washing them down with several half-pints of lunchtime lager. The thyme has stayed with me and now I never make a shepherd's pie without it.

About 6 tablespoons/90ml vegetable oil
A 2-in/5-cm stick of cinnamon
1 medium-sized onion, peeled and very finely chopped
2 teaspoons/10ml peeled and finely grated fresh ginger
7 cloves garlic, peeled and very finely chopped
2 lb/900g minced (ground) lamb
1–3 fresh hot green chillies, finely chopped (optional)
½ teaspoon/2.5ml ground turmeric
Salt
¼ teaspoon ground allspice
¼ teaspoon ground nutmeg
¾ teaspoon/4ml dried thyme
3 tablespoons/45ml chopped fresh green coriander (Chinese parsley) or regular parsley
1½ tablespoons/22ml lemon juice
Freshly ground black pepper
A 1-lb/450-g aubergine (eggplant)
1 lb/450g fresh tomatoes
1½lb/675g waxy potatoes, boiled in their jackets and cooled

For baking, I use a medium-sized lasagna dish or a large gratin dish. A large, not-too-deep casserole pot may be used instead. The measurements, roughly, should be 9 × 10 × 2in/23 × 25 × 5cm. I line the bottom of my pie dish with aubergine (eggplant) and tomatoes, thus making this a true one-pot meal.

Prepare the meat

Heat 3 tablespoons/45ml of the oil in a large frying pan or a wide pot over a medium flame. When hot, put in the cinnamon stick. Stir once and add the onion. Stir and fry until the onion is golden brown. Add the ginger and garlic. Stir and fry for another minute. Now put in the lamb, green chilli, turmeric and 1¼ teaspoons/6.25ml salt. Break up the lumps of meat and fry, stirring frequently, for 4–5 minutes. Add 4 tablespoons/60ml/¼ cup water and bring to a boil. Cover, lower heat, and simmer gently for 45 minutes. Remove the cover. Add allspice, nutmeg, ¼ teaspoon thyme, parsley, lemon juice and some freshly ground black pepper. Stir and dry off any remaining liquid on a higher flame. Spoon off and discard any fat that may have accumulated.

Prepare the vegetables

Preheat the grill (broiler).

Cut the aubergine (eggplant) into half, crosswise, and then cut each half lengthwise, into ½–¾-in/1.5–2-cm-thick slabs. Brush one side of the slabs with about 1 tablespoon/15ml oil. Dust lightly with salt and black pepper. Turn the slabs over. Brush the second sides with 1 tablespoon/15ml oil and dust lightly with salt and pepper. Place in a single layer under the grill (broiler). Cook on one side until medium-brown in colour. Turn the pieces over and brown them on the second side. Remove from the grill (broiler).

Cut the tomatoes crosswise into thin round slices.

Peel the potatoes and cut them crosswise into thin, even rounds (as thin as you can manage without crumbling the potatoes – anywhere under ¼in/6mm in thickness).

Previous Page
TOP: SPINACH AND LETTUCE SALAD WITH A LEMONY DRESSING. BOTTOM: A KIND OF SHEPHERD'S PIE

To assemble

Preheat the oven to 425°F/220°C/Gas Mark 7. Line a baking dish (see note above) with the aubergine (eggplant) slices, overlapping them if necessary. Lay the tomato slices over the aubergine (eggplant), overlapping them neatly. Sprinkle lightly with salt, black pepper, and ¼ teaspoon thyme. Cover the tomatoes with the meat, spreading it out evenly. Cover the meat with neatly overlapping slices of potatoes, arranging them rather like the scales of a fish. Brush the potatoes with about 1 tablespoon/15ml oil, and then dust lightly with salt, black pepper and the remaining ¼ teaspoon thyme. Place in the oven and bake for 30–35 minutes, or until the potatoes have browned a bit. Serve hot.

SPINACH AND LETTUCE SALAD WITH A LEMONY DRESSING
Serves 6

This nice, large salad is very pleasantly lemony.

For the Greenery

1 medium-sized head of any lettuce of your choice, its leaves well-washed and patted dry
About 5–6oz/140–180g well-washed and drained spinach leaves
1 spring onion (scallion), washed and trimmed

Tear up the lettuce and spinach leaves into big pieces and put in a bowl. Cut the spring onion (scallion) into 1-in/2.5-cm lengths and then cut each piece, lengthwise, into fine long slivers. Add the slivers to the salad bowl. Just before serving, pour in as much of the following dressing as you need to moisten the greens. Toss.

For the Dressing

1 tablespoon/15ml red wine vinegar
1 tablespoon/15ml lemon juice
½ teaspoon/2.5ml salt
Freshly ground black pepper
4fl oz/120ml/½ cup olive or salad oil

Combine the vinegar, lemon juice, salt and black pepper in a bowl and mix. Beat in the oil with a fork. Taste for seasonings. Beat dressing once again just before pouring over the salad.

ONE GOOD THING INSIDE ANOTHER

TOMATOES STUFFED WITH MINCED (GROUND) MEAT
COURGETTES (ZUCCHINI) WITH GARLIC
MATCHSTICK POTATOES WITH SESAME SEEDS

Stuffing vegetables may sound like tedious work, but, where tomatoes are concerned, it is no trouble at all. I cut a cap off the tomatoes and then use a grapefruit spoon to scoop out the insides. You could use an ordinary teaspoon: just be careful not to perforate the skin.

Sometimes I stuff the tomatoes with minced (ground) lamb – at other times, a mixture of veal and beef. It is a good idea to drain the cooked meat of all fat before stuffing. The stuffing can be made even a day ahead of time and refrigerated. If you do, reheat it and drain away the fat shortly before stuffing, otherwise the meat tends to dry out.

You can have your tomatoes stuffed before your guests arrive. Pop them into a preheated oven about 12 minutes before you sit down to eat.

The matchstick potatoes with sesame seeds, garlic, red chilli, lemon and sugar are a delectable combination of sweet, sour, salty, hot and nutty flavours, so typical of many parts of east and south Asia. They complement the tomatoes and also may be made ahead of time. (If I make them *too* far ahead of time, they just get gobbled up by every passing member of the family!) I serve them at room temperature.

Cook the courgettes (zucchini) just before you sit down to eat. You can do the salting, draining and drying off in advance. Cut your garlic and have it ready too. Cooking this dish is a snap and can be done as the tomatoes are baking.

TOMATOES STUFFED WITH MINCED (GROUND) MEAT

Serves 4

I was raised on stuffed tomatoes. Of course, we grew them in our garden and plenty of them too. They were red-ripe and full of flavour when we got ready to eat them. We grilled them to go with our breakfast eggs, we made our own fresh tomato juice to have for a mid-morning snack, we made our own ketchup, we made tomato stews, and cooked all kinds of vegetables, from beetroot (beets) to turnips, with them.

The largest, shapeliest tomatoes were reserved for stuffing. They made the perfect containers. I vary my stuffings just as my mother did and now include some made with meats not served to us as children – beef and veal.

3 tablespoons/45ml vegetable oil
1 medium-sized onion, peeled and finely chopped
1 teaspoon/5ml peeled and finely grated fresh ginger
6 cloves garlic, peeled and crushed to a pulp
¾lb/340g minced (ground) beef
¾lb/340g minced (ground) veal
Salt
¼ teaspoon ground allspice
⅛ teaspoon ground cloves
⅛ teaspoon ground nutmeg
⅛ teaspoon ground cinnamon
1 teaspoon/5ml dried oregano
1 tablespoon/15ml lemon juice
A few dashes Tabasco Sauce
Freshly ground black pepper
4 tablespoons/60ml finely chopped fresh parsley
4 large well-shaped tomatoes, each weighing about 12oz/340g

Opposite
TOMATOES STUFFED WITH MINCED (GROUND) MEAT, SERVED WITH COURGETTES (ZUCCHINI) WITH GARLIC, AND MATCHSTICK POTATOES WITH SESAME SEEDS

Heat the oil in a frying pan over a medium flame. When hot, put in the onion. Stir and fry until golden brown. Put in the ginger and garlic. Stir and fry for a minute. Put in the minced (ground) meats, 1 teaspoon/5ml salt, the allspice, cloves, nutmeg, cinnamon and oregano. Stir and fry the meat for 4–5 minutes, breaking up the lumps as you do so. Put in 4 tablespoons/60ml/¼ cup water and bring to a boil. Cover, lower heat, and simmer gently for 45 minutes. Remove cover, put in the lemon juice, Tabasco, black pepper and 3 tablespoons/45ml parsley. Turn heat up and dry off the remaining liquid, stirring as you do so. Spoon off any fat that may have accumulated.

Meanwhile, cut caps off the tomatoes at the stem end. Save the caps. Spoon out all the pulp (you can use it in some soup), being careful not to break the tomatoes' skins. Sprinkle the inside lightly with salt. Rub the salt in. Now turn the tomatoes upside down and leave them to drain for about 20 minutes or more.

Preheat the oven to 400°F/205°C/Gas Mark 6.

When the meat is cooked, stand the tomatoes right side up. Sprinkle them again very lightly with salt and black pepper. Now stuff each tomato with the meat: do not overstuff as the skins might crack. Put the caps back on and bake the tomatoes for 10–12 minutes, or until they just begin to wrinkle.

Remove the caps. Sprinkle the remaining 1 tablespoon/15ml parsley over the open tops and serve.

COURGETTES (ZUCCHINI) WITH GARLIC

Serves 4

I like courgettes (zucchini) cooked simply. Here, the young vegetables are stir-fried in hot oil with a little garlic. They are superb.

1½lb/675g smallish courgettes (zucchini) (each about 6in/15cm long)
Salt
3 tablespoons/45ml vegetable oil
2 cloves garlic, peeled and very finely chopped
Freshly ground black pepper

Trim away the courgette (zucchini) ends and cut each in half lengthwise. Using a teaspoon, scrape away all the seeds. Now cut them crosswise, into ⅓-in/1-cm segments. Put in a bowl. Sprinkle with 1 teaspoon/5ml salt and mix well. Set aside for 20 minutes. Drain and pat dry.

Heat a wok or cast-iron frying pan over a high flame. When hot, pour in the oil. Put in the garlic. Stir once or twice. Put in the courgettes (zucchini) and brown lightly. Keep stirring or turning so all the sides can brown a little bit. Cook for about 3–4 minutes this way. The courgettes (zucchini) should not be allowed to get too limp. Taste for salt, adding more as needed. Add freshly ground black pepper and serve.

MATCHSTICK POTATOES WITH SESAME SEEDS

Serves 4

I can munch on these potatoes all by them-selves (in fact, I often serve them with drinks), but they are very good served with grilled (broiled) chicken, stuffed and baked tomatoes and even grilled or baked fish. They are crunchy, slightly hot, slightly sour and slightly sweet. And very good.

1 medium-sized onion, peeled and coarsely chopped
2 cloves garlic, peeled
A ½-in/1.5-cm cube of peeled ginger
1 dried hot red pepper, crumbled
1 teaspoon/5ml ground cumin seeds
2 teaspoons/10ml lemon juice
4 medium-sized potatoes
Enough vegetable oil to have ½in/1.5cm in a big frying pan
1 tablespoon/15ml sesame seeds
¾–1 teaspoon/4–5ml salt
Freshly ground black pepper
1 teaspoon/5ml sugar

Put the onion, garlic, ginger, red pepper, cumin and lemon juice into the container of an electric blender or food processor. Blend until smooth, pushing down with a rubber spatula if necessary.

Peel the potatoes and cut into ⅛-in/3-mm slices. Stack the slices together and cut into strips the same thickness. (If not cooking immediately, put the strips in water, then drain and pat them dry.)

Heat the oil in a large frying pan over a medium flame. When hot, put in as many potatoes as will fit in easily. Stir and fry until golden and crisp. Remove with a slotted spoon and leave to drain spread out on paper towels. Do all the potatoes this way.

Remove all but 4 tablespoons/60ml of oil from the frying pan. Put the sesame seeds into the hot oil. Stir and fry until they begin to brown or pop. Pour in the mixture from the blender or food processor. Stir and fry slowly until the mixture has browned and is quite dry. This is important. Now put in the fried po-tatoes, salt, pepper and sugar. Mix, breaking up the spice clumps and spreading them about. Remove with a slotted spoon and serve hot or at room temperature.

COOKING FOR A DOZEN – GIVE OR TAKE A FEW

BUTTERFLIED LEG OF LAMB WITH TWO PEPPERS
GRILLED (BROILED) SPRING ONIONS (SCALLIONS)
CARROT AND SULTANA (RAISIN) SALAD FLAVOURED WITH
SESAME SEEDS
RICE WITH MOREL MUSHROOMS AND SWEET RED PEPPER

When you're expecting a goodly number of people for dinner, this is an exquisite – and stretchable – meal to serve them. You can feed 8 people or 12 people just as easily. Leftovers, if there are any – taste even better the next day. The only thing that doesn't keep is the spring onions (scallions), but then, you need grill just the number you need.

The lamb and spring onions (scallions) may be grilled outdoors in the summer or indoors when the weather is less cooperative.

The sweet and sour carrot salad may be made well in advance. The rice can be cooked just before guests arrive and then left in a warming oven.

I love this pepper-encrusted lamb with a passion. It is moist and tender inside and crunchily spicy on the outside. I carve it against the grain – diagonally. Its spicy taste is well balanced by the earthiness of the mushrooms, the sweetness of the carrot salad and the meltingly soft spring onions (scallions).

BUTTERFLIED LEG OF LAMB WITH TWO PEPPERS

Serves up to 12 people

An easy dish to put together, the lamb here may be barbecued or baked in the oven. According to your preference, you may cook the meat rare, medium or well-done. I like it when it is faintly pink in the middle and nicely browned on the outside.

Ask the butcher to 'butterfly' two whole legs of lamb for you. This involves removing the two bones inside the leg and then cutting the meat open so it lies flat, rather like a very large, irregular steak. Make sure that all the outside fat and the parchment-like fell on the leg is removed as well. If the butcher has not done this, do it yourself at home.

The meat needs to be marinated overnight.

Two legs of lamb, butterflied, with most of the outside fat and parchment-like fell removed
3fl oz/80ml/⅓ cup lemon juice
2 teaspoons/10ml salt
5 cloves garlic, peeled and crushed to a pulp
2 teaspoons/10ml finely grated peeled fresh ginger
1 teaspoon/5ml dried thyme
1 teaspoon/5ml well-crushed (use a mortar and pestle) dried rosemary
2 tablespoons/30ml black peppercorns
3 whole dried hot red peppers
5 tablespoons/75ml olive oil

Lay the butterflied legs out on a large plate or plastic tray and prod well on both sides with the tip of a sharp knife.

Combine the lemon juice, salt, garlic, ginger, thyme and rosemary in a bowl and mix. Dribble half of this mixture over one side of the lamb, spreading it out evenly and pushing it into the knife-holes. Turn the meat over and do the same with the other half of the mixture. Put the meat and all juices in a large bowl. Cover well and refrigerate overnight or longer.

Take the meat out of the refrigerator 3–4 hours before you sit down to eat. Spread it out again on a large plate or plastic tray.

Put the black pepper and hot red pepper into the container of a spice grinder. (I use a clean coffee grinder. You could instead use a mortar and pestle.) Grind coarsely. Sprinkle half of this mixture over one side of the lamb and pat it onto the meat so it adheres. Rub half of the olive oil over the meat. Turn the lamb pieces over and do the same with the other half of the pepper mixture and the remaining half of the olive oil. Set aside and allow the meat to come to room temperature.

The meat takes 45 minutes–1 hour to cook, longer if you want it well done. Preheat your oven accordingly to 500°F/260°C/Gas Mark 9.

Lay the meat out on a rack set over a baking tray, and put it in the upper third of the oven. Cook the meat for 20–30 minutes (20 for rare, 30 for medium) and then turn the meat over and cook again for another 20–30 minutes. Take the meat out of the oven and let it rest for about 15 minutes. Slice the meal slightly diagonally into thinnish slices.

GRILLED SPRING ONIONS (SCALLIONS)

Serves 12

Our cook in India used to bury small onions in the hot ashes of our stove. They would emerge slightly crisp on the outside and meltingly soft inside. I had forgotten about this very special treat until very recently when I ate at a Mexican restaurant in San Antonio, Texas. There, on the menu, were grilled spring onions (scallions). I ordered them immediately and found them to be second cousins to the ash-baked onions of my childhood. They had been rubbed with oil and then grilled over mesquite wood. I do mine rather simply, under the grill (broiler) in the kitchen.

24 spring onions (scallions)
About 3 tablespoons/45ml olive oil
Salt

Previous Page
CLOCKWISE FROM THE TOP: RICE WITH MOREL MUSHROOMS AND SWEET RED PEPPER, CARROT AND SULTANA (RAISIN) SALAD FLAVOURED WITH SESAME SEEDS, BUTTERFLIED LEG OF LAMB WITH TWO PEPPERS AND GRILLED (BROILED) SPRING ONIONS

Preheat the grill (broiler)

Trim the spring onions (scallions) so they are about 6in/15cm in length. (You do not need the very tops of the green sections.) Brush with oil and lay in a grilling (broiling) tray. Sprinkle very lightly with salt and place under the heat. When lightly browned, turn them over with tongs and brown the other side. Serve hot.

CARROT AND SULTANA (RAISIN) SALAD, FLAVOURED WITH SESAME SEEDS
Serves 12

5 tablespoons/75ml sultanas (golden raisins)
15 medium-sized carrots, trimmed and peeled
3 tablespoons/45ml finely chopped fresh parsley
¾ teaspoon/4ml salt
6 tablespoons/90ml vegetable oil
2 tablespoons/30ml whole yellow mustard seeds
3 tablespoons/45ml sesame seeds
2 tablespoons/30ml lemon juice
Freshly ground black pepper

Put the sultanas (raisins) in a bowl. Pour very hot water over them and leave them to soak for 2 hours. Drain.

Grate the carrots. (It is very easy to do this in a food processor if you happen to have one; otherwise grate by hand.) Put the carrots and drained sultanas (raisins) into a large bowl. Add the parsley and salt. Toss.

Heat the oil in a smallish frying pan over a medium-high flame. When hot, put in the mustard seeds. As soon as the mustard seeds begin to pop – this just takes a few seconds – put in the sesame seeds. Stir them about till they start to pop or brown. Empty the contents of the frying pan – oil and spices – over the carrots. Add lemon juice and black pepper. Toss and taste for seasonings.

RICE WITH MOREL MUSHROOMS AND SWEET RED PEPPERS
Serves 8–12

The dark spongy morel is much loved by all members of my family. Unfortunately, it is quite expensive. So I tend to use it sparingly. I have used a mere 12 dried ones in this recipe. If you feel like really splurging you could double the number. If you cannot find morels, substitute any other good-quality dried mushroom such as Italian *porcini*, Chinese sliced oyster mushrooms or Japanese shiitake mushrooms.

12 good-sized dried morel mushrooms (see note above)
Long-grain rice (use basmati, if available), measured to the 1¾-pint/1-litre/4 cup level in a glass measuring jug
5 tablespoons/75ml vegetable oil
1 smallish onion, peeled and cut into very fine half-rings
½ of a sweet red pepper, cut into ¼-in/6-mm dice
2pt 3fl oz/1.3 litre/5⅓ cups chicken broth or stock, home-made or canned
2 teaspoons/10ml salt – or to taste

Rinse off the mushrooms and soak in 2 cups of hot water for 30 minutes or until soft. Cut in half lengthwise, rinse under running water and pat dry. Wash the rice in several changes of water. Drain. Cover with water and leave to soak for 30 minutes. Drain.

Heat the oil in a large, wide, heavy pot over a medium-high flame. When hot, put in the onion. Stir and fry until lightly browned. Put in the morels and red pepper. Stir gently for 30 seconds. Put in the rice and turn the heat to medium. Stir and sauté the rice for 2–3 minutes. Now put in the chicken broth and salt. Bring to boil. Cover tightly, turn the heat to very low and cook for 25 minutes.

Stir gently before serving.

BEAUTIFUL BASICS

GLORIOUS KEBAB-BURGERS
PEAS WITH MUSHROOMS AND ONIONS
POTATOES BAKED WITH GARLIC

Contrary to what you may think, we do eat hamburgers – and we love them too, specially when they're thick and juicy.

I have worked out a mouthwatering Indian variation of the ordinary burger – I season it with a lightly sautéed mixture of onion, garlic, ginger and green chillies! With it I serve green peas and garlicky baked potatoes. This all makes for a very simple, but quite delicious meal.

GLORIOUS KEBAB-BURGERS
Serves 4

I may have made up this dish, but it was my husband who christened it. It is the best of 'fast food' and a true cross between fine kebab and juicy American hamburger.

Green chillies vary so much in their strength. I used one smallish *jalapeño* for this dish and it was just right. You will need perhaps 5–6 of the very slender chillies found in most Asian stores.

With this recipe, you can make 4 large hamburgers, 5 medium-sized or 6 small ones. The small ones are ideal for putting in a bun or between two slices of rye toast (with a thin slice of onion and some ketchup).

1 tablespoon/15ml peanut, groundnut or corn oil
A small (2½-oz/75-g) onion peeled and finely chopped
1 *jalapeño* pepper, very finely chopped (with seeds) or 5–6 fresh hot green chillies
2 teaspoons/10ml peeled and finely grated fresh ginger
3 cloves garlic, peeled and crushed to a pulp
1½ lb/675g lean minced (ground) beef
½ teaspoon/2.5ml salt
Freshly ground black pepper

Heat the oil in a non-stick frying pan over a medium flame. When hot, put in the onion. Stir and fry until the onion just begins to brown at the edges. Add the *jalapeño* and stir for a minute. Add the ginger and the garlic and stir for another minute. Turn off the heat.

Put the meat in a bowl. Add salt, black pepper and the mixture from the frying pan. Mix gently, but without compacting the meat too much.

Put a large cast-iron frying pan to heat over a medium-high flame. (If you do not have one, use any other large frying pan, lightly brushed with oil.) Form 4 patties with a light hand and when the frying pan is very hot, slap them on to its hot surface. When one side is nicely browned, turn the hamburgers over and brown the second side. When the second side has browned, turn the hamburgers over again. Turn the heat down a bit and cook the hamburgers to the desired doneness, turning them over now and then for even cooking. You can test their doneness with the point of a knife. (I like mine cooked through, but just barely.) Serve immediately.

PEAS WITH MUSHROOMS AND ONIONS
Serves 4

There is nothing to this dish. I threw it together one day in the country when my husband and I realized that we'd both forgotten to shop for a green vegetable. We always keep peas in the freezer for making cream of pea soup. Two packets were still there. They were pulled out and used to good effect.

Two 10-oz/285-g packets frozen peas
2 small onions, peeled
2 cloves garlic, peeled
20 medium-sized fresh mushrooms
6 tablespoons/90ml olive oil
Salt
Freshly ground black pepper to taste

Cook the peas according to the package instructions, but without salt. Drain and rinse under cold water. Set aside.

Cut the onions in half lengthwise and then crosswise into fine half-rings. Chop the garlic very finely.

Cut the mushrooms crosswise, stems and all, into not-too-thin slices.

Heat the oil in a frying pan over a medium-high flame. When hot, put in the onion and garlic. Stir and fry for a minute or more until the first signs of browning appear. Put in the mushrooms. Stir and fry for another minute. Add the peas, salt and black pepper. Mix and let the peas just heat through, lowering the flame if necessary.

POTATOES BAKED WITH GARLIC
Serves 4

I use an oval gratin dish to bake these potatoes. It happens to be enamelled cast iron, so it can first sit on the fire and then go into the oven. It is about 11in/27cm long and 8in/20cm at its widest. A round gratin dish or a shallow flame-proof casserole dish would also be quite suitable.

4 tablespoons/60ml peanut, groundnut, corn or olive oil
1 small (2½-oz/75-g) onion, peeled and chopped
2 cloves garlic, peeled and chopped
2 lb/900g potatoes, peeled and cut into ¼-in/6-mm thick rounds and put into a bowl
1 teaspoon/5ml salt

Freshly ground black pepper

Preheat the oven to 400°F/205°C/Gas Mark 6. Heat the oil in the gratin dish over a medium flame. When hot, put in the garlic and onion. Stir and fry until they turn slightly brown. Turn off the heat. Empty the contents of the gratin dish – oil and seasonings – over the sliced potatoes in the bowl. Add salt and pepper. Toss.

Cover the bottom of the still-oily gratin dish with slightly overlapping rows of potato slices. Any oil or seasonings that remain in the bowl should be emptied over the potatoes. Cover with a lid or foil and bake for 50 minutes–1 hour or until potatoes are soft.

Pour out and discard any extra oil. Either serve in the gratin dish itself or transfer neatly to a warm serving dish.

TASTY LESSONS FROM MEDIEVAL MONGOLS

KOREAN-STYLE BEEF
SPINACH WITH AN AROMATIC DRESSING
PERKY, PUNGENT GREEN SALAD
RICE COOKED WITH RAW PEANUTS

It was in the Middle Ages that invading armies of Mongols (a name that somehow is always associated with the word 'hordes') taught Koreans how to eat beef – to cut it into thin strips and barbecue over small braziers.

To this day, cattle ranches thrive on southern Cheju Island and every single town in the country is studded with restaurants that allow diners to grill their own marinated beef strips at the table and to gobble them down the second they are cooked. I have been in many of these smoke-filled rooms, working my way in through the almost blinding haze. The aroma of the slightly sweetened meat is overpoweringly tantalizing. It draws one into the recesses of the restaurant like a magnet.

Here, I've changed the Korean recipe only inasmuch as I cook the meat in a heated cast-iron frying pan instead of over an open fire. It is still excellent and has the added advantage of being very manageable. With the meat, I serve two Korean specialities – blanched spinach, seasoned with aromatic sesame oil and a special, very spicy green salad. Rice calms the palate and complements the beef. The ideal beverage to serve with this meal is cold lager. If you can find a Korean or Japanese beer easily, it just adds to the fun.

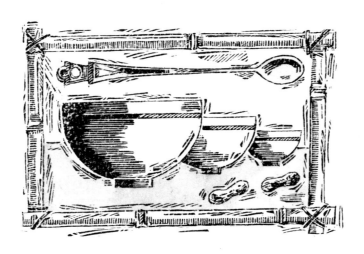

KOREAN-STYLE BEEF
Serves 6

The Koreans marinate strips of rib meat and then barbecue them over a live flame. They eat this with plain rice and lots of hot, garlicky pickles. Instead of rib meat, I have used steak – the better the quality of steak, the better this dish will be. Instead of barbecuing the meat, I cook these strips of beef in a very hot cast-iron frying pan.

1¾lb/800g beef fillet, rib fillet or sirloin steak about 1in/2.5cm thick
1½ tablespoons/22ml sugar
4 cloves garlic, peeled and mashed to a pulp
3 tablespoons/45ml soy sauce
4 spring onions (scallions), sliced into thin rounds all the way up their green sections
2 tablespoons/30ml oriental sesame oil
2 tablespoons/30ml vegetable oil

Cut the beef diagonally into very thin slices. Put in a bowl. Rub with the sugar and set aside for 10 minutes. Add the garlic, soy sauce, spring onions (scallions) and sesame oil. Rub this in too and set aside for 15 minutes or longer.

Heat a large cast-iron frying pan on high heat until it is very hot. Brush lightly with oil. Lay strips of meat in it in a single layer. When brown, turn the pieces over and quickly do the other side. Remove and put in a warm serving dish. Do all the pieces this way and serve immediately.

CLOCKWISE FROM THE TOP: SPINACH WITH AN AROMATIC DRESSING, KOREAN-STYLE BEEF, PERKY, PUNGENT GREEN SALAD, RICE COOKED WITH RAW PEANUTS

SPINACH WITH AN AROMATIC DRESSING
Serves 6

This dish is served at room temperature. You may make it several hours ahead of time and refrigerate it. Remove it from the refrigerator a little ahead of time to take off the chill.

2 lb/900g fresh spinach leaves, well-washed and drained
4 tablespoons/60ml soy sauce
3 tablespoons/45ml oriental sesame oil
¾ teaspoon/4ml sugar
1 tablespoon/15ml distilled white vinegar
Freshly ground black pepper

Heat a large pot of water over a high flame. When boiling, drop in the spinach. Drain it as soon as it wilts. Rinse out under cold water to preserve the colour and then squeeze out as much liquid as you can, by pressing small amounts between your two palms. Put in a bowl.

In a small bowl, combine the soy sauce, sesame oil, sugar, vinegar and black pepper. Mix. Throw over the spinach and toss, separating the leaves as you do so.

A PERKY, PUNGENT GREEN SALAD
Serves 6

I make this salad with crisp cos (romaine) lettuce only because that is how our local Korean restaurant does it. It is uncommonly good – and quite unusual.

A good-sized head of cos (romaine) lettuce or any other crisp lettuce (about 10oz/285g)
2 tablespoons/30ml soy sauce
1 clove garlic, peeled and crushed to a pulp
1 tablespoon/15ml oriental sesame oil

4 teaspoons/20ml distilled white vinegar
½ teaspoon/2.5ml sugar
¼ teaspoon cayenne pepper

Break the lettuce leaves into a bowl. Combine all the remaining ingredients in a cup and mix. Throw the dressing over the salad just before eating and toss.

RICE COOKED WITH RAW PEANUTS
Serves 6

Koreans make this dish with soy bean sprouts. Unlike the more readily available mung bean sprouts, these are fairly firm in texture, specially their seed end. They can actually be bitten into. One can generally buy them at Chinese grocers – they look like mung bean sprouts, only larger. But they cannot always be found. Once, when I was in a rush and did not have the six days to sprout them myself, I decided to use peanuts. Raw peanuts. Peanuts are, after all, a legume too. I soaked them overnight and rubbed their skins off. They made an exceedingly pleasant addition to the rice. Ideally, Japanese rice should be used. It has a stickier texture. If you cannot find it, any long-grain rice will do.

½ cup raw peanuts
Long-grain rice, measured to the 15-fl oz/425-ml/2 cup level in a glass measuring jug

Soak the peanuts overnight in a bowl. Next day, rub off their skins in the water. As you rub them, try splitting each peanut into its two natural halves. Pour off the skins and the water. Drain thoroughly, making sure all the skins are discarded.

Put the rice in a bowl and wash in several changes of water. Drain. Cover with fresh water and leave to soak for 30 minutes. Drain.

Combine peanuts, rice and 1pt/570ml/2⅔ cups water in a heavy pot. Bring to a boil. Cover very tightly and cook over a very low flame for 25 minutes.

WHEN CARDAMOM REIGNS

PERFUMED LAMB SMOTHERED IN ITS OWN JUICES
SWEET AND SOUR AUBERGINES (EGGPLANT)
RICE WITH BROAD BEANS (LIMA BEANS)
AND FRESH DILL

It is a pity that cardamom is not used more in the Western world to flavour meat and rice dishes. Scandinavians do use it when they make biscuits and cakes, but that is as far as it goes. Of all the spices in the world, cardamom is perhaps the most romantically aromatic. Cinnamon may have a strong aroma, but it is dark and heavy, nothing like the silvery, almost ethereal quality of cardamom. If I were to compare the flavours and aromas of spices to violins (only a violinist's wife would venture to make such an absurd comparison) I would definitely classify cardamom as the Stradivarius of spices. Its scent, like the tone of a good Stradivarius, is clear, clean and unmistakably magical.

The lamb in this meal is seasoned almost entirely with cardamom pods. It is an unusual dish, with a haunting flavour. To balance it, I serve one of my favourite cardamom-flavoured rice dishes – a kind of casserole of rice, frozen broad beans (baby lima beans), and fresh dill, and a baked dish of sweet and sour aubergine (eggplant), perked up with lemon juice and cumin seeds.

PERFUMED LAMB SMOTHERED IN ITS OWN JUICES

Serves 6

It is always such a pleasure to find a dish that has a multi-layered, complex taste, but is a result of a single, quite inspired idea.

Take this dish. When you eat it you may well wonder how it has been prepared. Is it braised? Is it baked? What are the seasonings?

Well, it is boiled – very simply – with just two spices, cardamom and black pepper. Once the lamb is tender, the boiling liquid is cooked down and the meat is left glistening in its own juices. The dish comes from an old, traditional recipe from the state of Sindh, now in Pakistan. Very few people know of it. The Sindhis who do, treasure it, eating it whenever they need something soothing, reassuring and delectable.

I find that the cut of meat that is best for this dish is lamb shoulder, with the bone in. The meat stays very moist if the bone and some of the fat is left attached to the meat. You can easily buy shoulder chops ¾-in/2-cm thick and have the butcher cut them through the bone for you into 1½–2-in/4–5-cm pieces.

Even though it is not traditional to put any hot red peppers in this dish, I sometimes throw in two whole red ones for just a little extra zing!

3 lb/1.35kg lamb shoulder chops, with bone, cut into 1½–2-in/4–5-cm squares
25 whole cardamom pods
1 tablespoon/15ml whole black peppercorns
2 whole, dried red hot peppers (all tied loosely in cheesecloth)
1¼ teaspoons/6.5ml salt (or to taste)
Freshly ground black pepper

Combine the lamb, the cheesecloth bag with the cardamom pods, whole peppercorns and red peppers, and salt, plus 15fl oz/425ml/2 cups water in a wide, heavy pot. Bring to a boil. Cover, turn the heat down, and simmer for

about an hour or until the meat is tender. (This dish may be cooked up to a day ahead of the time up to this point. Reduce the liquid just before you serve in order to keep the meat moist and juicy.)

Take the cheesecloth bag out of the pot, squeezing its juices back in. Discard the bag. Raise the heat and boil most of the liquid in the pot away, stirring the meat round gently as you do so. There should be a few tablespoons of liquid left at the end. The meat should turn darker, glistening as it is rolled around in its juices. Sprinkle freshly ground black pepper over the top. Stir the meat in its own juices again and serve.

SWEET AND SOUR AUBERGINES (EGGPLANT)

Serves 6

Here, overlapping slices of aubergine (eggplant) are placed in a baking dish to make this one of the prettiest and tastiest aubergine (eggplant) dishes I have ever eaten. I use the slim, long, pinkish-mauve aubergines. If you cannot find them, use the large oval ones. Just cut them crosswise into rounds.

Bake the aubergines (eggplants) in the same dish you use to serve them. I use an oval dish that is about 10in/25cm long and about 2½in/6.5cm high. But you could just as easily use a square or rectangular dish.

2½lb/1.125kg aubergines (eggplants)
6–8 tablespoons/90ml–120ml vegetable oil
Salt
Freshly ground black pepper
3 tablespoons/45ml lemon juice
2 tablespoons/30ml sugar
1 teaspoon/5ml ground roasted cumin seeds (see page 189)
¼ teaspoon cayenne pepper (optional)

Preheat the grill (broiler). Cut the aubergines (eggplants), somewhat diagonally into ⅓-in/1-cm thick oval slices. Brush generously on both sides with oil. Sprinkle each side lightly with salt and pepper as well. Put the slices, as many as will fit in a single layer, in a grilling

---

Previous Page
CLOCKWISE FROM THE TOP: RICE WITH BROAD BEANS (LIMA BEANS) AND FRESH DILL, PERFUMED LAMB SMOTHERED IN ITS OWN JUICES, SWEET AND SOUR AUBERGINES (EGGPLANT)

(broiling) tray and cook on both sides until golden red. Do all the aubergines (eggplants) this way. Turn off the grill (broiler).

Preheat oven to 350°F/180°C/Gas Mark 4.

Mix together the lemon juice, sugar, cumin, cayenne, ½ teaspoon/2.5ml salt and some black pepper. Arrange the aubergine (eggplant) slices in a baking dish in slightly overlapping rows. When the bottom is covered with a layer of slices, dribble a third of the lemon juice mixture over them and spread it out evenly with your fingers. Cover the first layer with two more layers, coating each one with the lemon mixture. Cover the baking dish with foil and then bake in the preheated oven for 20 minutes.

RICE WITH BROAD BEANS (LIMA BEANS) AND FRESH DILL

Serves 6

I first learned of this combination from a Persian friend. All the ingredients here blend with the harmony of a perfect risotto.

Long-grain rice (basmati, if you can find it), measured to the 15-fl oz/425-ml/2 cup level in a glass measuring jug

A 10-oz/285-g packet of frozen broad beans (baby lima beans) or 10oz/285g fresh broad beans.
3 tablespoons/45ml vegetable oil
3 whole cardamom pods
1 small onion, peeled and then cut into very fine half-rings
1 firmly packed cup chopped fresh dill
1 teaspoon/5ml salt
1pt/570ml/2⅔ cups chicken broth or stock, home-made or canned

Wash the rice in several changes of water. Drain. Soak in a bowl of fresh water for 30 minutes. Drain and leave in a strainer.

Cook the frozen beans according to package instructions, but only for half the time suggested. If using fresh beans, cook until they are half done. They should retain a little firmness. Drain.

Heat the oil in a heavy, medium-sized pot over a medium flame. When hot, put in the cardamom pods and stir once. Quickly put in the onion. Stir and fry until the onion browns. Put in the drained rice, the dill, the drained beans and salt. Stir and fry for about 2 minutes or until the rice turns translucent. Turn the heat down a bit if it starts to stick. Now add the chicken broth and bring to a boil. Cover tightly, turn the heat to very low, and cook for 25 minutes.

HEARTY FARE

BEEF WITH MUSHROOMS
RICE WITH YELLOW SPLIT PEAS AND GARLIC
TURNIPS COOKED WITH TOMATOES

These days, especially in big cities, one can buy most root vegetables at all times of the year. Sometimes I think this is such a shame. It has taken away all the romance out of going down into a root cellar and foraging in cold sacks and bins for precious vegetables.

I always think of turnips that way, as something to have when the weather turns chilly. This meal, consisting of hearty beef stew, rice cooked in a casserole with yellow split peas, and turnips stewed with tomatoes is devised for such days, which can occur anytime from autumn until spring.

The beef is specially good when cooked with dried morel mushrooms. Their spongy caps soak up the beefy broth while lending their own earthy, buttery flavour to the beef. They require a brief soaking, but have a wonderful dark taste and a firm texture. If you cannot find them, use ordinary white mushrooms. The rice that accompanies this meal is flavoured with cinnamon and cloves, spices that all Indians insist have special chemical properties that warm the insides of our bodies. All in all, it is a superb meal, worthy of a full-bodied red wine.

BEEF WITH MUSHROOMS

Serves 8

I normally make this dish with the easy-to-find white mushrooms. But when I want to splurge a bit, I buy the very expensive dried morels. If you decide on the dried variety, wash them well under running water and then soak them for an hour or so until they are soft. Rinse them again thoroughly, making sure you remove the grit that is invariably inside them.

This dish can be made ahead and reheated.

8–9 tablespoons/120–135ml vegetable oil
4 lb/1.75kg boneless stewing beef, cut into 1½-in/4-cm cubes
1 teaspoon/5ml whole cumin seeds
A 2-in/5-cm stick cinnamon
8 whole cardamom pods
8 whole cloves
1¼pt/720ml/3 cups plain yoghurt, lightly beaten until smooth
4 cloves garlic, peeled and finely chopped
A 1-in/2.5-cm cube fresh ginger, peeled and finely chopped
1 tablespoon/15ml ground coriander seeds
1 teaspoon/5ml cayenne pepper (optional)
Salt
2 good-sized onions (9-oz/250-g) peeled and sliced into thin half-rings
12–18 dried morel mushrooms (see above)
Freshly ground black pepper

Heat 3 tablespoons/45ml of the oil in a large wide pot over a high flame. When hot, put in as many pieces of meat as will fit easily in a single layer and brown quickly. Remove with a slotted spoon and put in a bowl. Brown all the meat this way. Add another tablespoon of oil to the pot and put in the cumin, cinnamon, cardamom and cloves. Stir once and put in the meat and the accumulated juices from the bowl as well as the yoghurt, garlic, ginger, coriander, cayenne, ½pt/275ml water and 1¼ teaspoons/6.5ml salt. Bring to a simmer. Cover, lower the heat and simmer gently for 1½ hours or a bit longer, until the meat is tender.

Meanwhile, heat 5 tablespoons/75ml oil in a frying pan over a highish flame. Put in the onions. Fry them, stirring, until they turn reddish-brown in parts. Put in the mushrooms and stir for a minute or two until they lose their raw look. Add about ½ teaspoon/2.5ml salt and some black pepper. Stir to mix and turn off heat.

When the meat is tender, put in the onion-mushroom mixture. Stir and mix. Turn up the heat to medium-high for 10 minutes or so to thicken the sauce a bit. Stir gently a few times as you do this.

NB   The large whole spices are not meant to be eaten.

RICE WITH YELLOW SPLIT PEAS AND GARLIC

Serves 8

3oz/85g/½ cup yellow split peas
Long-grain rice, preferably basmati, measured to the 1¼pt/720ml/3 cup level in a glass measuring jug
3 tablespoons/45ml oil
A 1-in/2.5-cm stick of cinnamon
1 bay leaf
3 cloves
3 cloves garlic, peeled and finely chopped
1 small (2-oz/60-g) onion, peeled and cut crosswise into very fine half-rings
1½ teaspoons/7.5ml salt

Rinse the split peas and soak for one hour. Drain.

Wash the rice in several changes of water. Drain. Put in a bowl, cover well with water and leave to soak for 30 minutes. Drain.

Heat the oil in a heavy pot over a medium flame. When hot, put in the cinnamon, bay leaf and cloves. Stir once and put in the garlic and onion. Stir and fry until the onion and garlic begin to brown. Add the drained rice, split peas and salt. Stir for a couple of minutes or until the rice turns translucent. Add 1¾pt/1 litre/4 cups water and bring to a boil. Cover tightly, turn the heat to very low and cook for 25 minutes.

NB The whole spices should be removed before serving.

TURNIPS COOKED WITH TOMATOES

Serves 6–8

Even people who look upon turnips with a doubtful eye seem to enjoy this particular dish very much.

2 lb/900g medium-sized turnips
¾lb/340g tomatoes
3 tablespoons/45ml vegetable oil
1 teaspoon/5ml whole cumin seeds
¾pt/425ml/2 cups chicken broth or stock (home-made or canned)
Salt
¼ teaspoon ground turmeric
⅛–¼ teaspoon cayenne pepper

Peel the turnips and cut them into quarters (or sixths, depending on size), lengthwise.

Chop the tomatoes coarsely.

Heat the oil in a good-sized pot over a medium-high flame. When hot, put in the cumin seeds. Ten seconds or so later, put in the turnips and tomatoes. Stir for a minute. Put in the stock, salt to taste if needed, turmeric and cayenne. Bring to a simmer. Cover, turn the heat low and simmer gently for 15–20 minutes or until the turnips are tender. Just before serving, heat the turnips in their liquid, lift them out with a slotted spoon, and place in a warm serving dish. Turn the heat up and reduce the liquid until you have only about 5fl oz/150ml left. Pour this over the turnips and serve.

THE NORTH WIND DOTH BLOW

OUR FAVOURITE PORK CHOPS
DELICIOUS AROMATIC CABBAGE
NEEPS AND TATERS

There are times when the weather is brisk and one has been splitting wood (one's husband actually does that), skiing or ice-skating (one's children do that), planting bulbs and trees in the garden (one does that oneself), or even working devilishly hard at the office, when one longs for a steaming-hot, hearty meal.

Here is one of my favourites – perfect for late autumn and winter. Of all the ways I cook pork chops, this remains the most popular with my family and friends. (One friend from India even cabled her arrival date with a request for these chops!) It is a made-up recipe. I made it up myself a long time ago, borrowing bits from the cuisines of India and China.

The cabbage – which goes so well with pork – is a simplified version of a dish we ate as children in India, while the 'Neeps and Taters' – mashed swede (rutabaga) and potatoes – are from Scotland. I picked up the recipe from a crew member while we were shooting the film *The Assam Garden* in the United Kingdom.

The pork chops take about an hour to cook. Both vegetable dishes can be made while the chops simmer.

OUR FAVOURITE PORK CHOPS

Serves 6

I probably made this dish up about twenty years ago and my family has been eating it ever since. Somehow I'd never written the recipe down. But my daughter Sakina had. Just before going off to Vassar College, she had taken to following me around the kitchen, jotting down the recipes for everything she knew she would miss and want to cook at college. So when it came to writing this book, I found myself in the unusual position of borrowing this recipe back from her.

12 thin-cut pork chops (loin chops are best)
2 tablespoons/30ml vegetable oil
6 whole cloves
1 bay leaf
A 1-in/2.5-cm stick of cinnamon
1 whole hot dried red pepper (optional)
1 carrot, peeled and sliced into ¼-in/6-mm thick rounds
1 medium-sized onion, peeled and chopped
4 tablespoons/60ml/¼ cup soy sauce
2 tablespoons/30ml sugar

Heat the oil in a very large frying pan over high heat (I use my 14-in/35-cm cast-iron pan). When hot, put in as many pork chops as will fit in a single layer and let them brown. Turn them over and brown the second side. (They will be quite uncooked at this stage). Remove and put in a bowl. Brown all the chops this way.

Put the cloves, bay leaf, cinnamon and red pepper into the remaining oil in the frying pan. Stir once or twice until the bay leaf darkens a bit. Now put in the carrot and onion. Stir and let them brown for a minute. Turn the heat down. Put in the browned chops, any liquid that may have accumulated in the bowl, the soy sauce, sugar and enough water to come three-quarters of the way up the chops. Bring to a simmer. Cover (I use a wok lid) and simmer for 50–60 minutes or until chops are tender. During the period, turn the chops around several times, taking those on the bottom and laying them on the top, so the flavour penetrates all equally. Adjust the heat so that at the end of the cooking time, just a little thick sauce is left clinging to the meat.

NB The large whole spices are not meant to be eaten.

DELICIOUS AROMATIC CABBAGE

Serves 6

Even if you have never cared for cabbage, you will love this dish.

A medium-sized cabbage (about 2½lb/1.25kg)
2 medium-sized onions, peeled
3 tablespoons/45ml vegetable oil
½ teaspoon/2.5ml whole cumin seeds
½ teaspoon/2.5ml whole fennel seeds
4 teaspoons/20ml sesame seeds
1 teaspoon/5ml salt – or to taste

Remove the coarse outer leaves of the cabbage. Cut the cabbage in half through its core. Remove the core. Cut the two halves into very fine long shreds. You could use a mandolin to do this or, if you like, use the shredding gadget on a food processor.

Cut the onions into half lengthwise and then cut the halves crosswise into fine half-rings.

Heat the oil in a large, wide pot over a medium flame. When very hot, put in the cumin and fennel seeds. As soon as the spices turn a shade darker (this takes just a few seconds), put in the sesame seeds. Stir them for a second and put in the onions. Stir and fry the onions until they are brown at the edges. Now put in the cabbage and salt. Stir and fry for a minute. Cover tightly and turn heat to low. Cook for 2–3 minutes or until the cabbage wilts. Uncover. Turn the heat back up a bit, stirring and frying the cabbage for another 5 minutes. The cabbage can brown very slightly if you like: it tastes good that way.

Previous Page
OUR FAVOURITE PORK CHOPS, SERVED WITH DELICIOUS AROMATIC CABBAGE, AND NEEPS AND TATERS

NEEPS AND TATERS

Serves 6

I first had this Scottish dish – a glorious mixture of mashed swedes (yellow turnips, also called rutabagas) and potatoes – in Wales, where I was shooting *The Assam Garden* with Deborah Kerr. One member of our film crew came from Scotland and, knowing how interested I was in all culinary delights, had decided to cook us a Scottish meal complete with an authentic Cock-a-leeky soup, Haggis, and these 'Neeps and Taters'. We dutifully accompanied the superb meal with an extraordinary amount of peaty, unblended whisky and lots of song, the former leading quite naturally to the latter!

I have added only 1 tablespoon/15ml butter to the mashed mixture. You could add up to four times that amount if you so wish.

We like to mash our 'neeps and taters' coarsely, so I throw them into an electric mixer together. If you want a creamier texture, mash the turnips first, then add the potatoes and all other ingredients.

A large swede (yellow turnip or rutabaga) about 2½lb/1.25kg, peeled and cut into 1-in/2.5-cm dice
5 good-sized boiling potatoes, about 2 lb/900g, peeled and cut into 1-in/2.5-cm dice
1 tablespoon/15ml butter
1¼–1½ teaspoons/6.25–7.5ml salt
Freshly ground black pepper
Freshly ground nutmeg

Drop the diced turnips into a large pot of boiling water. Cover and boil on a medium-low flame for about 20 minutes. Lift the cover and put in the potatoes. Cover again and boil on a medium-low flame for another 20–30 minutes or until vegetables are tender. Drain.

Mash vegetables by hand or whip with an electric beater, adding the butter, salt, black pepper and a dash of nutmeg as you do so. The texture may be left a bit coarse.

This dish may be kept hot in a double boiler or, if you do not have one, by putting it in a metal bowl, covering it with foil, and putting the bowl in a large pot of gently simmering water that comes only three-quarters of the way up the sides of the bowl.

A FEAST FOR ALL TIMES

THE BEST ROAST PORK, ECUADOR-STYLE
GARLICKY CRANBERRY CHUTNEY
ASPARAGUS AND GREEN BEANS WITH SESAME SEEDS
RICE AND POTATO CASSEROLE

Parents teach children. Children teach parents. The give and take in our family, as in most others, continues and covers all fields. This meal is dedicated to my daughter Meera, who not only taught me how to cook the pork, but has, over the years, sent me recipes from as far away as Beijing. (Yes, she called collect. One Chinese recipe cost me $80 *and* was worth it!)

Meera cooks fast – and effortlessly. She flits around in the kitchen, talking of this and that, her mind never – seemingly – fully on the food. And yet, just when I think, 'Now, she is going to forget to rub the marinade on the second side of the meat,' she, in mid-sentence about some wonderful eighteenth-century brass candle-holder, flips the meat over casually and begins massaging it with the marinade, and meanwhile, there has been no pause at all in her soft, earnest conversation.

When she first made the pork for us, we were all amazed not so much by its gentle citrus flavour, which we expected, as by the buttery tenderness of the meat itself. Pork – roasts and chops – can get quite dry if not properly handled. The braising liquid here – and the jabbing with the point of a knife – tenderizes it, making it very succulent indeed. I like to time it so that the roast finishes cooking just as my guests are having their first drink. I then take it out of the oven and leave it sitting in a warm spot.

The chutney I serve with the pork is somewhat unusual. It is made in short order from a can of cranberry sauce. I make it well in advance and keep it in a jar in the refrigerator. The rice can be started just before guests arrive and then left to finish on its own. (You just have to remember to turn the heat off.) The only thing I make at the last minute are the vegetables. I cut them up beforehand and leave them soaking. Just before we eat, I drain them and set them to cook. They take only 5 minutes.

THE BEST ROAST PORK, ECUADOR-STYLE

Serves 8

Tangy and meltingly soft, the meat here is partly braised and partly roasted.

Ask your butcher to give you either a boneless pork shoulder or else the rib end of the pork shoulder with the ribs removed. The latter, which I buy frequently, is a long strip, and once the bones are removed and the meat tied up, it looks rather like a Swiss roll (jelly roll). The butcher should remove the rind.

5 cloves garlic, peeled and crushed to a pulp
1 medium-sized onion, peeled and very finely chopped
6fl oz/178ml/¾ cup orange juice
4fl oz/60ml/¼ cup lemon juice
2 teaspoons/10ml red wine vinegar
1 teaspoon/5ml ground sage
1 teaspoon/5ml sugar
2 teaspoons/10ml salt – or to taste
Freshly ground black pepper
Boneless pork shoulder for roasting (see note above), weighing about 4 lb/1.75kg

Combine the garlic, onion, orange juice, lemon juice, vinegar, sage, sugar, salt and pepper. Mix.

Preheat the oven to 400°F/205°C/Gas Mark 6.

Put the pork into a casserole-type pot, the less fatty side facing up. Take a small knife with a sharp point and jab the roast all over, riddling it with holes. Take half of the prepared juice mixture and pour it over the meat, rubbing it into the slits. Turn the meat over and do the same on the second side. Leave the second side facing up. Cover the pot and put it in the oven. Bake for 45 minutes. Take the pot out of the oven and remove the lid. Pour out all but about 4 tablespoons/60ml of the liquid in the pot. Return the casserole to the oven, and cook, uncovered, for another 45 minutes, basting occasionally with the juices that were removed. The roast should brown lightly on the outside. Slice and serve.

GARLICKY CRANBERRY CHUTNEY

Makes ¾pt/425ml/2 cups

One day I reached into a kitchen cupboard to take out a can of chicken broth and by mistake pulled out, and without looking, opened a can of jellied cranberry sauce. It was not anywhere near Thanksgiving Day and my mind was very far from cranberries. The can, however, was open and could not be wasted, so I invented a quick and delicious cranberry chutney to go with the pork roast we were eating. Here it is:

A 1-in/2.5-cm cube of fresh ginger, peeled
3 cloves garlic, peeled and very finely chopped
4fl oz/120ml/½ cup apple cider vinegar or distilled white vinegar
4 tablespoons/60ml/¼ cup sugar
⅛ teaspoon cayenne pepper, or to taste
A 1-lb/450-g can or jar of jellied cranberry sauce
½ teaspoon/2.5ml salt
Freshly ground black pepper

Cut the ginger into paper-thin slices. Stack the slices together and cut them into very thin slivers.

Combine the ginger slivers, garlic, vinegar, sugar and cayenne in small pot. Bring to a simmer. Simmer on a medium flame for about 15 minutes or until there are about 4 tablespoons/60ml of liquid left (excluding the solids). Add the cranberry sauce, salt and pepper. Mix and bring to a simmer. It will be a bit lumpy, but that is fine. Simmer on a gentle heat for about 10 minutes. Cool. Put in a jar and refrigerate. This will keep for several days.

Previous Page
CLOCKWISE FROM THE TOP: RICE AND POTATO CASSEROLE, GARLICKY CRANBERRY CHUTNEY, THE BEST ROAST PORK, ECUADOR-STYLE, ASPARAGUS AND GREEN BEANS WITH SESAME SEEDS.

ASPARAGUS AND GREEN BEANS WITH SESAME SEEDS

Serves 6–8

We planted an asparagus patch in our country garden a few years ago, but find that we never seem to produce enough of the vegetable to satisfy us. So we have developed ways to stretch our meagre yield. One of these ways is the addition of green beans. It *is* a bit like cheating, I suppose. The two vegetables are similar in size, colour and texture, and the beans end up by soaking in some of the flavour of the asparagus for which I'm always very grateful. My husband calls this combination 'as-beanagus'.

1 lb/450g asparagus of medium thickness
1 lb/450g green beans
3 tablespoons/45ml olive oil
2 tablespoons/30ml sesame seeds
4 tablespoons/60ml/¼ cup chicken broth or stock, home-made or canned
2 tablespoons/30ml dry vermouth
½ teaspoon/2.5ml salt
Freshly ground black pepper

Trim away the hard, woody part of the asparagus. Peel the bottom third of each spear and then cut each spear into 2-in/5-cm lengths. Trim the green beans and cut them into 2-in/5-cm lengths as well. Soak both vegetables in cold water for 10 minutes. Drain.

Heat the oil in a large frying pan over a medium flame. When hot, put in the sesame seeds. As soon as the sesame seeds start to pop, or darken, put in the asparagus and green beans. Stir gently until they turn bright green. Add broth, vermouth, salt and pepper. Bring to a simmer. Cover and cook on a medium flame for 3–4 minutes or until the vegetables are tender. Remove the lid. Turn up the heat slightly and boil all the liquid away. Serve immediately.

RICE AND POTATO CASSEROLE

Serves 6–8

Here I combine two starches to make an exquisite, top-of-the-cooker 'casserole'.

Long-grain rice, measured to the 1¼pt/720ml/3 cup level in a glass measuring jug
3 tablespoons/45ml olive oil
1 teaspoon/5ml whole cumin seeds
1 smallish onion, peeled and cut into fine half-rings
1 good-sized potato, peeled and cut into ¼-in/6-mm dice
½ teaspoon/2.5ml dried sage
¼ teaspoon dried marjoram
28fl oz/880ml/3½ cups chicken broth or stock, home-made or canned
4fl oz/120ml/½ cup dry vermouth
About 1½ teaspoons/7.5ml salt – or to taste

Wash the rice in several changes of water. Drain. Leave to soak in fresh water to cover for 30 minutes. Drain.

Heat the oil in a large, wide pot over a medium-high flame. When hot, put in the cumin seeds. Stir once and put in the onion. Stir and fry until the onion starts to brown. Put in the potatoes. Stir and fry until the potatoes just start to brown. Put in the rice, sage and marjoram. Stir and fry for 2 minutes, lowering the heat if the rice starts to stick. Put in the stock, vermouth and salt. Bring to a boil. Cover, turn the heat to very low and cook for 25 minutes.

SOUPS
AND LIGHT FARE

There are times when all one wants to eat is a soup – something soothing and warming if it is winter, crunchy and cooling if it is summer.

I have always loved soups. When we were little and unwell, my mother would sit at our bedsides and spoon-feed us 'soup-toast'. Bits of freshly made toast were broken off, dunked into a steaming soup, usually a clear chicken or lamb broth with just a few droplets of the naturally rendered fat floating on the surface. One felt so wanted and cared for. Perhaps it is this memory that makes me fill my refrigerator with containers of clear broths. No chicken or duck carcass, lamb or veal bone is thrown away. I collect them all and once a week throw them into a pot along with an onion studded with whole cloves, a few bay leaves, a carrot or two, celery, and other odd vegetables left over (such as outer leaves of lettuce, tomato halves, unused onion tops and parsley stems). Through the week, we all drink this soup from mugs (I still dunk toast in it), or I use the broth as a base to make dozens of other, heartier soups.

In India, I grew up with a meaty, clove-scented split pea soup, tomato soup made from our own garden-grown vegetables, pea soup made with our own very sweet peas, a delicious cashew nut and lamb soup and a very delicate almond soup. Now as I travel around the world, I have added to my repertoire a lime-flavoured lentil and prawn (shrimp) soup from the Philippines, a hearty American corn chowder from the Midwest, an Indo-Portuguese kale soup flavoured with bacon, a Thai chicken noodle soup flavoured with peanuts and a deliciously crunchy cold soup from Ecuador filled with a julienne of raw vegetables and prawns (shrimp) that is as good if not better than a wonderful salad.

These soups may be eaten with thin crisp toasts, with warmed slices of crusty breads, with sandwiches, or quite simply, with green salad on the side.

In this chapter, I have also put in a couple of other simple meals – meals which do not feature soups and can be prepared quickly and easily.

One includes a pasta dish – linguini topped with an exquisite sauce of fresh tomatoes – and the other has as its main course a lovely, sesame encrusted corn bread, which I serve with a simple spinach and bacon salad and some tea and coffee.

GLORIOUS CORN

EASY CORN CHOWDER
CRISP TOASTS

I cannot help but get sentimental every time I eat corn chowder. You see, a long time ago, over two decades ago, a young man and I were sitting in a neighbourhood restaurant in Greenwich Village, eating a simple bowl of this chowder, when he was suddenly seized by the desire to propose to me. The restaurant was very noisy. He insists that I said 'Yes', I insist that I said nothing at all, or 'Hmm', at best.

At any rate, the facts are that the restaurant (the Limelight) is no more, but we are married.

EASY CORN CHOWDER
Serves 6

There is nothing quite as soothing as a bowl of steaming corn chowder on a cool day. There are hundreds of recipes for this all across America. Mine is probably one of the simplest. It is also quite delicious. You could serve it for lunch with crisp toasts or with a crusty loaf of bread or as part of a larger meal.

2½ pints/1.4 litres/6 cups chicken broth (home-made stock or canned broth) salted to taste
1 bay leaf
1 medium-sized onion, peeled and chopped
¾lb/340g potatoes, peeled and cut into ⅓-in/1-cm dice
1 carrot, peeled and cut into ⅓-in/1-cm dice
½ teaspoon/2.5ml dried thyme
3½ teacups corn, either taken off the cob or frozen
4fl oz/120ml/½ cup single (heavy) cream

In a large pot, combine the broth, the bay leaf, onion, potatoes, carrot and thyme. Bring to a boil. Cover, lower the heat, and simmer for 25 minutes. Remove the bay leaf and leave simmering while you do the next step.

Into the container of a food processor or blender, put the corn and 1½ cups of the soup, including some of the cooked vegetables in it. Stop and start the machine a few times so the corn kernels get broken up and the cooked vegetables get somewhat mashed. Pour this mixture back into the soup. Add the cream and bring to a simmer. Cook gently for 5 minutes. Taste for salt.

CRISP TOASTS

You can make these out of almost any bread. If it is slightly stale, so much the better. Italian loaves, French bread – all may be used: I happen to like unseeded rye bread. I cut it quite thin and allow about 3 slices per person. The toasts may be made several hours ahead of time and stored either in a large airtight plastic container or in a plastic bag.

18 ¼-in/6-mm thick slices bread

Preheat the oven to 275°F/140°C/Gas Mark 1. Spread the slices out in a single layer in a baking tray. Bake for about 10 minutes or until slices are golden and quite crisp.

Overleaf
EASY CORN CHOWDER SERVED WITH CRISP TOASTS

WARM AND NOURISHING

CREAMED SPINACH AND SPLIT PEA SOUP
THICKLY SLICED WHOLEWHEAT BREAD
RADISHES AND SPRING ONIONS (SCALLIONS)

I serve this thick split pea soup, all laden with nourishing greens, with thick slices of crusty wholewheat bread and lots of radishes and spring onions (scallions) on the side to nibble on at will. Choose any dark bread that you like. You can either make it yourself or pick from the many available. These days bread shops and health food shops carry bread encrusted with sunflower seeds and others made with wheatgerm or a mixture of rye, corn and wheat. I have even had breads which contained whole coriander seeds or aniseed, which were quite delicious. If you cut these in thick slices and put them in a basket, the bread not only looks pretty but tastes wonderful with this soup.

CREAMED SPINACH AND SPLIT PEA SOUP

Serves 4

All kinds of vegetables may be combined to make cream soups. Here I've put spinach and watercress together with potatoes and split peas to make a rich, tasty and nourishing soup.

3oz/85g/½ cup green split peas, picked over, washed and drained
A 10oz/285g package of frozen spinach
1 large bunch (5oz/140g) watercress
1 medium-sized onion, peeled and chopped
1 medium-sized potato, peeled and chopped
8 canned plum tomatoes plus about 4fl oz/ 120ml/½ cup juice from the can
1¾ pints/1 litre/4 cups chicken broth or stock, home-made or canned
8fl oz/237ml/1 cup single (heavy) cream
1 tablespoon/15ml lemon juice
A few dashes of Tabasco Sauce (optional)
Salt
Freshly ground black pepper

Soak the split peas in water for an hour. Drain.

Combine the spinach, watercress, onion, potato, tomatoes, the tomato juice, chicken broth and split peas in a large pot. Bring to a boil. Cover, lower the heat and simmer for one hour. Pour liquid into an electric blender and blend until smooth. Add cream, lemon juice, Tabasco Sauce, salt to taste and black pepper. Mix. Taste for seasonings, adding more as you see fit.

RADISHES AND SPRING ONIONS (SCALLIONS)

Serves 4

I have a weakness for radishes. Remember that their smallest, pale green, inner leaves are very edible. Remove just the large, outer, dark green leaves, leaving the younger inside leaves still attached to the vegetable.

You will need at least 12 radishes and 8 spring onions (scallions). Wash the radishes well and arrange them on a plate with the trimmed and washed spring onions (scallions).

CHARMING INFLUENCES FROM PORTUGAL AND THAILAND

CALDO VERDE (KALE AND POTATO SOUP)
AN OPEN TUNA SANDWICH WITH A THAI DRESSING

I love soup and sandwich lunches. I usually have the two together (even in coffee shops, where I insist that the waiter serve me the two at the same time), though you could, of course, serve the soup first and follow it with the open sandwich. Goa, in India, was a Portuguese colony from the early sixteenth century until the 1960s. Its foods today are often a glorious blend of Mediterranean produce and that of coastal India. Some dishes, however, have been preserved in their pure Portuguese forms. This soup is one of them.

CALDO VERDE (KALE AND POTATO SOUP)

Serves 4–6

4 strips of bacon
2½ pints/1.5 litres/6 cups any meat or poultry stock, fresh or canned (you might need a little more for thinning out the soup)
4 medium-sized potatoes, peeled and coarsely chopped
1 medium-sized onion, peeled and coarsely chopped
2 firmly packed teacups (about 6oz/150g) coarsely chopped kale leaves
10 cloves garlic, peeled
Salt to taste
Freshly ground black pepper
1 tablespoon/15ml fruity olive oil

Turn the heat on under a large, wide, heavy pot, keeping it at medium-low. Spread out the strips of bacon and cook them slowly until they are crisp on both sides and have rendered all their fat. Remove the bacon strips with a slotted spoon, leaving all their fat behind. Spread the bacon strips on a paper towel to drain. Add the stock to the pot as well as the potatoes, onions, kale, garlic, salt and black pepper. Crumble just one of the bacon strips and add that as well. Bring to a boil. Cover, lower heat, and simmer gently for about 1¼ hours.

In as many batches as is necessary, pour the soup into the container of an electric blender and blend until smooth. Pour the soup back into the pot and thin it out if you think it necessary with some of the extra stock. Add salt if you need it and some black pepper.

Pour into a warm soup tureen or into individual bowls. Dribble a little olive oil over the top. Crumble the three remaining slices of bacon and sprinkle them over the top as well.

AN OPEN TUNA SALAD SANDWICH WITH A THAI DRESSING

Serves 4–6

This perky salad – Thai in its use of shallots, mint and lime – may be served on a bed of lettuce leaves or, as I often do, on individual slices of toasted bread. You may butter your bread slices very lightly before toasting them if you so wish. All sorts of bread may be used – white, wholewheat, rye or any mixture of grains that you like.

The salad may be made up to a day in advance, covered and refrigerated. It should be put on fresh toast at the very last minute. Allow each person 1–2 toasts, as you see fit.

If you cannot find shallots easily, use half a red onion. Cut it into very thin rounds and then quarter the rounds.

2 tablespoons/30ml long-grain rice
2 6½-oz/200g cans white tuna (in brine)
5 good-sized shallots (2oz/60g), peeled and sliced into thin slivers
1½ teaspoons/7.5ml sugar
1 teaspoon/5ml soy sauce
2 cloves garlic, peeled, lightly crushed and then chopped very finely
About 4 tablespoons/60ml fresh lime juice (or to taste)
¼ teaspoon cayenne pepper (or to taste)
Freshly ground black pepper
⅓ well-packed cup of chopped fresh mint plus extra sprigs for garnishing
4–8 slices of bread (see note above)
About ½ teaspoon/2.5ml unsalted butter for each slice of bread (optional)

Heat a small cast-iron frying pan over a medium flame. When hot, put in the rice. Stir and roast the rice until it turns light brown in colour. (A few grains may be darker, a few lighter, some may even pop.) Allow it to cool slightly and then grind in a clean coffee grinder.

Empty the tuna and all the liquid in the cans into a bowl. Flake the fish. Add the shallots, sugar, soy sauce, garlic, lime juice, cayenne, black pepper and chopped mint. Mix and taste for seasoning, adding anything more that you think is necessary.

Just before serving, butter one side of each slice of bread with about ½ teaspoon/2.5ml butter, and toast to golden in a toaster oven. If you do not have a toaster oven, preheat the grill (broiler) and put the bread directly on the hot tray to toast one side; butter the second side and toast it. Put some salad on each toast, garnish with a sprig of mint and serve.

HOT, SOUR AND NUTTY

THAI NOODLE SOUP

This soup, with its haunting medley of hot, sweet, sour, nutty and salty tastes, is a meal in itself. On my visits to Thailand, I so enjoy stepping into one of the many noodle shops whenever I want to rest and have a quick bite of something tasty. There are always so many varieties of fresh noodles to choose from – thick flat rice noodles, thin flour and egg noodles, thin round rice noodles and so on. The noodles are heated quickly in broth and then served with a topping of vegetables and bean sprouts. You are left to season the soup yourself – a ground red chilli paste, crushed peanuts, salty fish sauce and sugar sit at the table. You put in just as much as you want and it is all great fun. No accompaniment is served or needed, even though cold beer or lager on hot days is exceedingly pleasant.

THAI NOODLE SOUP

Serves 6

If you can find fresh Chinese lo-mein noodles, do use them. As a substitute, use good quality spaghettini. For the salty sauce, use any Thai or Vietnamese fish sauce (such as *nam pla*), if available. Otherwise, use soy sauce.

½lb/225g fresh Chinese lo-mein egg noodles (see above for substitutes)
1 teaspoon/5ml cayenne pepper
1 tablespoon/15ml distilled white vinegar
¼pt/150m/l½ cup fish sauce (see note above), or soy sauce
¾ cup unsalted, roasted or fried, shelled peanuts
Sugar
3¾ pints/2.24 litres/9 cups chicken broth or stock, home-made or canned, salted to taste
1 teaspoon/5ml grated lemon rind
About 25 green beans, cut into ¾-in/2-cm segments
2 cups washed and drained bean sprouts
½ lightly packed cup chopped fresh green coriander (Chinese parsley)

Bring a large pot of water to a rolling boil. Drop in the noodles, pulling them apart as you do so. When the water comes to a boil again, pour in a cup of cold water. Bring the water to a boil again and when it does, again pour in a cup of cold water. When the water comes to a boil yet again, drain the noodles and rinse them off under cold running water. (If using spaghettini, cook it according to package instructions, drain and rinse off under cold running water.)

Prepare all the seasonings and set them out on your table: mix the cayenne and vinegar and put it in a small bowl, the kind you might use for prepared English mustard – such bowls usually have their own Chinese spoons; put the fish sauce in a bowl; crush the peanuts coarsely in a mortar or clean coffee grinder for just a second or two and put in a third bowl; set out the sugar bowl.

Combine the chicken broth and lemon rind in a big pot and bring to a boil. Throw in the green beans and let them boil for a minute. Throw in the noodles, bean sprouts and green coriander (Chinese parsley). Let them heat through. Serve immediately, ladling the soup out into individual soup dishes.

Every diner is expected to season his own soup according to his liking with the hot cayenne sauce, the fish or soy sauce, the peanuts and the sugar. I rarely add more than ½ teaspoon/2.5ml sugar.

COOL (OR HOT) AND STUNNING

MINTY PRAWN (SHRIMP) SOUP, ECUADOR-STYLE

You have weekend guests in your house and you are going to serve a big dinner. What do you serve for lunch?

You want it to be light but impressive, simple to make, but with unforgettably enticing flavours. Try this soup from Ecuador. The first time I made it, I accidentally left out an ingredient – a small amount of chopped peeled tomatoes. We did not miss them. In fact, we all agreed that the soup could not be improved upon. It was quite perfect.

I serve this soup all by itself with some fresh fruit or a light fruit dessert to follow.

You can, of course, also serve this soup as part of a meal. I often serve it with The Best Roast Pork, Equador-Style (see page 127).

MINTY PRAWN (SHRIMP) SOUP, ECUADOR-STYLE

Serves 6–8

An Ecuadorian family has taken to camping in an antique store that my daughter Meera helps run for her boyfriend in New Jersey. The dozen or so members, all rather ample in girth, but not in height, sit on the side chairs, rock in the rockers, and very occasionally, buy an object or two which they promise to pay for 'later'. One day, in lieu of payment perhaps, they came in with a bowl of soup. This soup. They explained that it was an amazingly effective 'hair-of-the-dog' soup, perfect for hangovers. My daughter, who was not suffering from one, tasted it anyway and declared it to be delightful.

It is a most unusual soup, combining prawns (shrimp), orange juice, lemon juice, mint and raw vegetables with – would you believe it – tomato ketchup. Yet, the end result is light, cool, crisp, crunchy and *very* refreshing.

You can serve this soup hot or cold. The vegetables should be cut as thinly as you can manage. And once they're put into the soup, it should not be cooked again, though you may reheat it quickly if you so wish. You may make the soup several hours in advance and refrigerate it. Its flavour only improves.

1½lb/675g medium-sized prawns (shrimp)
6 tablespoons/90ml fresh orange juice
2 tablespoons/30ml fresh lemon juice
1 teaspoon/5ml red wine vinegar
3 tablespoons/45ml tomato ketchup
3 tablespoons/45ml finely chopped fresh mint
2 tablespoons/30ml fine slivers of lemon rind, 1in/2.5cm long
1 medium-sized (3½oz/100g) onion, peeled and cut crosswise into paper-thin half-rings
About half of a large (½-lb/225-g) green pepper, cut into the thinnest possible slivers, 2in/5cm long
1½ teaspoons/7.5ml salt
Lots of freshly ground black pepper

Bring 3¼ pints/2 litres/8 cups of water to a boil. Drop in the *un*peeled prawns (shrimp). Within 2 minutes or so, even before the water comes back to a boil, they will turn white, and cook through. Drain the prawns (shrimp) immediately, *saving* the boiling liquid. Let the prawns (shrimp) cool slightly and then peel and devein them. Save the skins.

Put the prawn (shrimp) skins back into the water that they were boiled in and bring to a boil. Lower the heat and simmer gently for 15 minutes. Strain the liquid, discarding the skins. Add the orange juice, lemon juice, vinegar, ketchup, mint, lemon rind, onion, green pepper, salt and pepper to the broth. Mix well and taste for seasoning. Put in the peeled prawns (shrimp) and stir.

This soup may now be covered, refrigerated and served cold up to 8 hours later; or it may be brought to a quick boil and served hot.

Previous Page
MINTY PRAWN (SHRIMP) SOUP, ECUADOR-STYLE

CELEBRATING SUMMER'S BOUNTY OF TOMATOES

LINGUINI WITH FRESH TOMATOES
STIR-FRIED CAULIFLOWER FLAVOURED WITH RICE GRAINS
AND VINEGAR
WATERCRESS AND CHICORY (BELGIAN ENDIVE) SALAD

Come July and August, every farmer's market and kitchen garden is bursting over with juicy, flavourful red, red tomatoes. They may, of course, be eaten out of hand with a tiny sprinkling of salt and pepper or put into salads or stir-fried with vegetables. They can also be made into a mouth-wateringly good, *uncooked* sauce for hot pasta.

On balmy summer days, we set out a table under the generous shade of a hoary sugar maple tree. The grass underfoot almost cries out for shoes to be kicked off.

This vegetarian pasta dish, served with quickly sautéed cauliflower and a perky watercress salad, is just ideal for an informal lazy summer's day.

LINGUINI WITH FRESH TOMATOES

Serves 4

This dish should be called the Navasky Linguini. It was invented for an editor friend who was under medical instructions at the time to eat most of his vegetables raw.

To peel and seed tomatoes, bring a large pot of water to a boil. Drop the tomatoes in for 10–15 seconds. Drain and peel them. Then cut the tomatoes in half, crosswise, and gently squeeze out and discard the seeds.

6 good-sized, red-ripe tomatoes, peeled, seeded and chopped (4 cups)
1 well-packed cup coarsely chopped fresh parsley
1 well-packed cup coarsely chopped fresh basil leaves
6 tablespoons/90ml olive oil
1 teaspoon/5ml whole yellow mustard seeds
6 cloves garlic, peeled and finely chopped
1 fresh, hot green chilli, minced – use less, if desired
Salt and freshly ground black pepper to taste
1 lb/450g linguini, freshly cooked at the last minute according to package instructions

Combine the tomatoes, parsley and basil.

Heat the oil in a frying pan over a medium flame. When hot, put in the mustard seeds. As soon as the mustard seeds begin to pop (this takes just a few seconds), put in the garlic. As soon as the garlic begins to brown, put in the green chilli. Shake the pan once and then pour the olive oil and spice mixture over the tomato mixture. Season with salt and pepper and toss. Empty the tomato mixture over freshly cooked linguini and toss again. Serve immediately.

STIR-FRIED CAULIFLOWER FLAVOURED WITH RICE GRAINS AND GINGER

Serves 4–5

In many regions of south Asia, small quantities of rice are used as a seasoning. In this dish, for example, rice grains are first dropped into hot oil where they explode like popcorn. The vegetable is then sautéed in this nuttily flavoured oil.

1 medium-sized head of cauliflower (about 2–2¼lb/900–1000g)
A 1-in/2.5-cm cube of fresh ginger, peeled
5 tablespoons/75ml vegetable oil
2 teaspoons/10ml yellow mustard seed
2 teaspoons/10ml uncooked rice grains
1–2 whole hot dried red peppers
1–5 whole fresh hot green chillies
¾–1 teaspoon/4–5ml salt
Freshly ground black pepper
4 tablespoons/60ml finely chopped parsley

Cut the cauliflower into small, delicate florets.

Cut the ginger into very thin slices and then the slices into very thin strips.

Keep a bowl of water near the stove.

Heat the oil in a wok over a medium-high flame. When hot, put in the mustard seeds and rice. As soon as they begin to pop (this takes just a few seconds), put in the red peppers and green chillies. Stir once, and put in the ginger. Stir once, and put in the cauliflower, parsley and salt. Stir and fry, adding a sprinkling of water every time the cauliflower threatens to brown. The cauliflower should cook in 5–8 minutes. It should be slightly crunchy, but cooked through.

WATERCRESS AND CHICORY (BELGIAN ENDIVE) SALAD

Serves 4

A large bunch watercress (weight about 5oz/140g)
A small head chicory (Belgian endive) or half a large one, weighing about 2½oz/75g
1 teaspoon/5ml Dijon-style mustard
1 teaspoon/5ml red wine vinegar
⅛ teaspoon salt
Freshly ground black pepper
2 tablespoons/30ml olive oil

Trim and wash the watercress. Pat dry.

Separate chicory (endive) leaves and cut into half crosswise. Cut each section lengthwise, into ¼-in/6-mm wide strips. Combine with the watercress in a bowl.

Put mustard in a small bowl. Add vinegar, salt and pepper. Mix. Beat in the oil, little by little.

Just before serving, beat the dressing once again and pour over the salad. Toss to mix.

VERY LIGHT AND VERY GOOD

A LIGHT MUSHROOM AND VEGETABLE SOUP, FULL OF FLAVOUR

PLAIN, STEAMED RICE, SEASONED WITH SPRING ONIONS (SCALLIONS) AND SESAME SEEDS

QUICK PICKLED RADISHES

HOT VINEGAR

If you are looking for a light, not fattening lunch, this is it. I make it often for our family. Sometimes we eat it all by itself, but at other times, I offer a little plain rice on the side, to give the meal some substance.

The rice, which is seasoned with sprinklings of very finely sliced spring onions (scallions) and some roasted sesame seeds, is best served in individual bowls so that each person may either dunk spoonfuls at a time in their soup or else eat mouthfuls of it as an accompaniment. The pickled radishes (which we all adore) should be passed along on the side: nibble on them at will. As for the hot vinegar, it is really a seasoning, small amounts of which can be added to the soup if you so desire. Every Chinese restaurant in India has a bowl of this condiment sitting at the table and, ever since childhood, I have come to depend upon it.

A LIGHT MUSHROOM AND VEGETABLE SOUP, FULL OF FLAVOUR

Serves 4–6

Any time is a good time for this soup, but our golden autumn, when the woods near us sprout wild mushrooms beside every fallen log, is best of all. I throw all these mushrooms into the pot, along with cupfuls of cut vegetables. If you do not have access to wild mushrooms, use whatever your markets carry, both fresh and dried. For this recipe, I have used a combination of ordinary fresh white mushrooms and dried Chinese black ones, as these are the most easily available. The only 'seasoning' I use – a trick learned from the Chinese – is sesame oil.

18 dried Chinese black mushrooms
1 lb/450g fresh mushrooms
3 tablespoons/45ml vegetable oil, preferably peanut or groundnut
2 tablespoons/30ml oriental sesame oil
Salt
Freshly ground black pepper
3¼ pints/2 litres/8 cups chicken broth or stock, home-made or canned
½lb/225 g green beans, trimmed and cut into 1-in/2.5-cm lengths
4 carrots, peeled and cut into rounds ⅛in/3mm thick
About 9oz/250g/3¾ cups very small, slim, cauliflower florets
2 teacups crisp bean sprouts (with the dark ends of their tails trimmed if you feel up to it)
4 spring onions (scallions), cut into very fine rounds all the way up their green sections

Rinse out the dried mushrooms and soak them in ¾ pint/425ml/2 cups of hot water for 30 minutes or until their caps are soft. Cut off and discard their hard stems. Cut the mushroom caps into halves or quarters depending upon size. Cut the fresh mushrooms lengthwise, into fine slices.

Heat the vegetable oil in a frying pan over a medium-high flame. When hot, put in the two types of mushrooms. Stir and sauté until the fresh mushrooms soften and begin to glisten. Add about ¼ teaspoon salt, some black pepper, and 1 tablespoon/15ml sesame oil. Stir to mix, and set aside.

About 8 minutes before you sit down to eat, bring the broth to a boil. Put in the green beans. Turn the heat down and simmer for 2 minutes. Put in the carrots and cauliflower. Bring to a boil. Turn the heat down again and simmer for 2 minutes. Now put in the bean sprouts, spring onions (scallions) and mushrooms (plus all accumulated liquid in the frying pan.) Bring to a boil. Turn the heat down and simmer for 1 minute. Taste for salt. Add the remaining 1 tablespoon/15ml sesame oil. Stir and serve.

PLAIN STEAMED RICE SEASONED WITH SPRING ONIONS (SCALLIONS) AND SESAME SEEDS

Serves 4

Long-grain rice measured to the 8fl-oz/237-ml/ 1 cup level in a glass measuring jug
2 spring onions (scallions), trimmed
2 tablespoons/30ml sesame seeds

Wash the rice in several changes of water. Drain. Cover well with water and leave to soak for 30 minutes. Drain.

Meanwhile, cut the spring onions (scallions) crosswise into paper-thin rounds. Put in a bowl of cold water and leave to soak for 1 hour.

Roast the sesame seeds by heating a small cast-iron frying pan over a medium flame, putting in the sesame seeds and stirring and cooking them till they are lightly browned. They tend to fly around as they roast, so you can put a loose cover over the pan.

Combine the rice and 10fl-oz/316ml/1⅓ cups water in a small pot. Bring to a boil. Cover very tightly. Turn the heat to very low and cook for 25 minutes. If left covered, and in a warm place, this rice will stay hot for at least 45 minutes.

Drain the spring onions (scallions). Put them in a teacloth or paper towel and gently squeeze out as much moisture as you can.

Put the rice in 4 individual bowls. Scatter the spring onions (scallions) over the top, and the sesame seeds on top of them. (Those who are eating mix the rice themselves before taking the first mouthful.)

QUICK PICKLED RADISHES

Serves 4

Try and buy radishes with their greens attached – they look so pretty. If you cannot find small radishes at all, but can find a slim, Japanese white radish about 1in/2.5cm in diameter, use about 7in/18cm of it. Peel it and cut it into ½-in/1.5-cm-thick rounds, then quarter the rounds.

12 radishes
½ teaspoon/2.5ml salt
1 teaspoon/5ml soy sauce
½ teaspoon/2.5ml oriental sesame oil

Trim away all the coarse outer leaves of the radishes, leaving at least one small tender leaf in the centre still attached. Trim away the 'tails' and wash the radishes well. Halve or quarter each radish lengthwise, depending on size. Sprinkle the salt over the cut pieces and rub it in. Spread the radishes out on a plate. Put another plate over them, to press them down, and put a small weight on the second plate. Set aside for 3–4 hours. Drain. Wash under running water and drain again. Pat dry with paper towels.

Put the radishes in a bowl. Pour the soy sauce and sesame oil over them and mix well.

HOT VINEGAR

Serves 4 or more

This keeps a week so you can make more and keep it in a jar. Just a few drops added to a soup gives it a delightful pungency.

4 tablespoons/60ml distilled white vinegar
¼ teaspoon salt, or to taste
1 fresh hot green chilli, cut into very thin rounds

Combine all the ingredients and set aside for 15 minutes or longer.

Previous Page
CLOCKWISE FROM THE TOP: QUICK PICKLED RADISHES, A LIGHT MUSHROOM AND VEGETABLE SOUP, FULL OF FLAVOUR, HOT VINEGAR, PLAIN STEAMED RICE SEASONED WITH SPRING ONIONS (SCALLIONS) AND SESAME SEEDS

AN ORIENTAL TOUCH

GREEN LENTIL SOUP WITH A FLAVOUR OF THE PHILIPPINES
SALAD OF GREENS AND FRESH FRUIT

What a superb soup this is – green lentils combined with prawns (shrimp), with a hearty flavouring of garlic, tomatoes and lime juice. You do not need much else. I serve a nice refreshing salad of greens and orange slices afterwards.

GREEN LENTIL SOUP WITH A FLAVOUR OF THE PHILIPPINES

Serves 6–8

There are many countries in southern and eastern Asia that delight in mixing various beans and split peas with fish and seafood. Just as in Virginia or Kentucky, where black-eyed beans may be cooked with ham hocks, in India, yellow split peas may be cooked with a fish head. If the Germans serve a split pea soup afloat with smoky sausage slices, the Filippinos serve a dish of mung beans dotted with freshly caught prawns (shrimp). The West already knows that the flavour of legumes marries well with smoked meats and poultry (just think of a cassoulet). The joys of combining legumes with seafood are just waiting to be discovered.

8 tablespoons/120ml olive oil
2 medium-sized onions, peeled and finely chopped
Dried green lentils, measured to the 12-fl oz/ 356-ml/1½ cup level in a glass measuring jug
3¼ pints/2 litres/8 cups chicken broth or stock, home-made or canned
½lb/225g medium-sized prawns (shrimp) (about 5½oz/150g when peeled)
6–7 cloves garlic, peeled and finely chopped
Salt
Freshly ground black pepper
1 lb/450g tomatoes, peeled (after dropping them into boiling water for 15 seconds) and finely chopped – canned tomatoes may be substituted
4 tablespoons/60ml finely chopped fresh parsley
Very thin rounds of fresh lime (or lemon)

Heat 3 tablespoons/45ml of the oil in a large, wide pot over a medium flame. When hot, put in the onions. Stir and fry until they get translucent and limp. Add the lentils and the chicken broth. Cook for about 40 minutes or until the lentils are tender.

Meanwhile, peel and devein the prawns (shrimp). Wash and pat dry. Cut each one into half lengthwise.

Heat the remaining 5 tablespoons/75ml oil in a frying pan over a medium flame. When hot, put in the garlic. Stir until it turns light brown. Add the prawns (shrimp). Stir and fry until they turn opaque and are just cooked through. Remove the frying pan from the fire. Take out leave all the oil behind. Put the prawns in a bowl, dust lightly with salt and black pepper, and toss. Put the frying pan back on the fire and toss. Put the frying pan back on the fire and heat the oil remaining in it. When hot, put in the chopped tomatoes. Stir and cook them until soft and a bit reduced, lowering the heat if necessary.

After the soup has cooked for 40 minutes, empty the contents of the frying pan into the soup pot. Cook for another 10 minutes. Add salt if you need it and some black pepper. Stir and turn off heat. Set aside as many prawn (shrimp) pieces as there are servings. If the soup is your main dish, people will surely have 2 helpings, so keep 2 prawn pieces aside for each person. Put the rest into the soup.

When ready to eat, heat the soup and ladle it into individual bowls. Sprinkle parsley over the top. Float a slice of lime in the centre. Place a piece of prawn (shrimp) on top of the slice of lime, and serve.

SALAD OF GREENS AND FRESH FRUIT
Serves 6

This dish reminds me so much of the cumin-flavoured, savoury fruit salads my mother used to make for us in India. Sometimes she used fresh guavas, and at other times a fruit that has come to be known in America as Chinese star-fruit (it looks like a yellow star when cut crosswise in slices). Vary the fruit with the season: bilberries (blueberries) are *very* good: you can throw some in with the oranges; peaches (peel and slice them at the very last minute); even hard, crunchy pears (also to be peeled and sliced at the very last minute). Cumin, through some mysterious magic of its own, draws out the very essence of the fruit.

1 smallish head of cos (romaine) lettuce (12oz/ 340g)
1 medium-sized orange
½ cup fresh bilberries (blueberries) in season
1 tablespoon/15ml red wine vinegar
1 tablespoon/15ml Dijon-style mustard
1 teaspoon/5ml roasted and ground cumin seeds (see page 189)
¼ teaspoon salt
Freshly ground black pepper
3fl oz/79ml/⅓ cup olive oil or other salad oil of your choice

Separate and wash the lettuce leaves. Pat or spin dry. Put in a salad bowl.

Peel the orange, making sure you remove all the white pith. Cut crosswise into ¼-in/6-mm thick slices. Cut each slice into 4 or 6 segments and put into the salad bowl.

If using berries, wash them and pat them dry. Throw them into the salad bowl as well.

Make the dressing
Put the vinegar and mustard, cumin, salt and pepper in a small bowl. Mix well. Just before serving, beat in the oil slowly with a fork. Pour over the salad and toss.

A VERY SPECIAL CORN BREAD

SPINACH AND BACON SALAD
COFFEE OR HOT TEA OR ICED TEA
GOLDEN SESAME CORN BREAD

There are times when one wants to eat a little something but not a whole lunch or dinner. Here is just such a meal. Have it before a roaring fire in the winter: set a small, pretty table near the hearth. In the summer, enjoy it under a shady tree: throw a checkered tablecloth on an outdoor table and bring out tall glasses of iced tea with sprigs of mint in them.

The corn bread may be eaten plain, or with butter or with sweet chutneys (try my Garlicky Cranberry Chutney on page 127).

SPINACH AND BACON SALAD

Serves 4–6

In order to keep this salad crisp, add the bacon and the dressing at the very last minute. The roasted cumin gives the dish a very fresh flavour.

8–10 rashers of bacon
10oz/285g fresh spinach

For the Dressing

1 tablespoon/15ml Dijon-style mustard
1 tablespoon/15ml distilled white vinegar
½ teaspoon/2.5ml ground roasted cumin seeds (see page 189)
¼ teaspoon/1.25ml salt, or to taste
Freshly ground black pepper
Dash of cayenne pepper, optional
6 tablespoons/90ml olive or other salad oil

Spread out the bacon slices in a grilling tray and grill (broil) on both sides until crisp. (You may cook the bacon in a frying pan or a microwave oven, if you so wish.) Drain well on paper towels and set aside.

Wash the spinach, breaking it off into leaves. Dry it. Tear large leaves into 2–3 pieces and put them all into a salad bowl.

Make the dressing: Put the mustard into a small bowl. Mix in the vinegar, cumin, salt, black pepper and cayenne. Beat in the olive oil a little bit at a time.

Just before serving, mix the dressing again and pour as much over the salad as you need to moisten it. Crumble the bacon and spread it over the top. Toss again.

ICED TEA

Makes 6 glasses

Even though I make my hot tea with loose tea leaves, I am not all that particular when I prepare iced tea. The reason is simple. Iced tea, invented on a very hot day in New Orleans just after the turn of the century, is really a glorious American lemonade. You might call it a tea-flavoured lemonade. The delicate aroma or taste of the tea is less important than the tang of the lemon and the clinking of ice-cubes in a tall glass. It is perfectly acceptable to use good quality tea bags. And it is very convenient.

As iced tea was invented in America, it is only natural that the best method of making it comes from America as well. Contrary to all rules of tea-making, iced tea is best when made not with boiling water but with ordinary tap water. It does not turn in the slightest bit cloudy, even if left sitting in the refrigerator for a whole day.

It is best to serve this tea with sugar syrup (sugar takes too long to melt in an icy glass) and lemon wedges (round slices look pretty but it is too hard to squeeze their juice out). It is customary to squeeze the juice of one (or two) wedges into the glass and then to drop the remaining wedge into the glass for added flavour. Iced tea is served in very tall glasses so they can hold not only a lot of tea but a lot of ice cubes. Special, long-handled teaspoons are used for stirring. You may have to improvise as best as you can.

To make the sugar syrup, combine 1 pound/ 450g castor sugar (superfine sugar) with about 1 pint/570ml/2½ cups water and heat over a medium-low flame until the sugar has melted. Cool and store in the refrigerator. Use as needed.

8 tea bags
About 42–48 ice cubes
2 lemons
6 sprigs of fresh mint, optional
Sugar syrup (see note above)

Snip off the paper tags on the tea bags with a pair of scissors and put the bags in a large jar. Add 2½ pints/1 litre/425ml/6 cups water from the tap (faucet) and stir. Cover loosely and refrigerate overnight or at least 12 hours.

When you are ready to serve, pour out the tea into 6 very tall glasses, leaving the tea bags behind. Add 7–8 ice cubes to each glass and stick a mint sprig into each of them as well. Cut each lemon into 6 wedges and put them on a plate. Pour the sugar syrup into a lipped syrup jar or milk jug. Pass the lemon wedges and sugar syrup around so people can help themselves to whatever they desire.

GOLDEN SESAME CORN BREAD
Serves 8

I suppose such things are bound to happen when a woman from India marries a man from America whose father comes from the southern state of Kentucky. This corn bread, a direct result of this pleasant cross-fertilization, is so amazingly good that we find ourselves eating it for lunch, dinner – and even with tea. It is slightly sweet, slightly sour (it has yoghurt in it), slightly hot (green chilli), slightly pungent (the ginger does that), and nutty from sesame seeds. Those who have eaten a freshly baked *handva*, a savoury cake from the Indian state of Gujarat, will easily recognize its ancestry.

I bake this in a cake tin and cut it into slices, but if you want to use a bun (muffin) pan, you should be able to divide the mixture into 12.

Green chillies vary so much in their heat. I used one *jalapeño* for this recipe and it was just perfect. If I were to use the slim long green chillies found in most Asian grocery stores, I might use 5–7. Just use your discretion here.

1 tablespoon/15ml plus 4 tablespoons/60ml/ ¼ cup peanut, groundnut or corn oil
1 tablespoon/15ml whole yellow mustard seeds
1 tablespoon/15ml whole sesame seeds
6oz/15g/1 cup corn meal
5oz/140g/1 cup plain (all-purpose) flour
3 tablespoons/45ml sugar
4 teaspoons/20ml baking powder
½ teaspoon/2.5ml salt
8fl oz/237ml/1 cup plain yoghurt, lightly beaten
2fl oz/60ml/¼ cup milk
1 egg, lightly beaten
1 fresh *jalapeño* pepper or 5–6 fresh hot green chillies, very finely chopped (with seeds)
2 teaspoons/10ml very finely grated, peeled, fresh ginger
2 tablespoons/30ml chopped, fresh green coriander (Chinese parsley)

Preheat the oven to 400°F/205°C/Gas Mark 6.

Pour 1 tablespoon oil into an 8 × 8 × 2-in/ 20 × 20 × 5-cm cake tin and heat over a medium-low flame. When very hot, put in the mustard seeds. As soon as they begin to pop, put in the sesame seeds. Stir them about for 10 seconds. Remove the tin from the fire. Spoon out the seeds and put them in a saucer. Some will remain clinging to the tin. This is as it should be. Leave them there. Just push what remain towards the bottom.

Combine the corn meal, flour, sugar, baking powder and salt in a bowl. Mix slightly. Add yoghut, milk, egg, *jalapeño* or chillies, ginger, green coriander (Chinese parsley) and 4 tablespoons/60ml/¼ cup oil. Stir gently and mix thoroughly.

Spoon the corn-bread batter into the cake tin. Scatter the seed mixture from the saucer over the top as evenly as you can. Bake for 25–30 minutes or until golden brown.

NB This bread is best served straight out of the oven. I cut it into squares or thick slices and put them in a bread basket lined and covered with a single large napkin. However, it can be made ahead of time, wrapped in foil and reheated in a 400°F/205°C/Gas Mark 6 oven for 10–12 minutes.

BRUNCHES AND TEAS

There is something so exquisitely relaxing about Sunday. One eases out of bed only when one wants to, the Sunday papers are at hand and Monday is a cloud still hidden behind the hills. One wants so much to see one's friends – but not, of course, before a very civilized hour – noon.

Brunch then, is the perfect meal. Nothing too complicated, mind you, as the sense of ease, comfort and well-being should continue through the course of the afternoon.

On the other hand, one could serve a leisurely tea instead, as I often do, starting around 4.30 or 5.00 pm, thus giving oneself even more time to drift around in one's night clothes.

By tea I mean 'English' tea – not 'high tea' which is a meal in itself and replaces dinner, but 'afternoon tea' at which the beverage, generally hot but now, succumbing to Americanization, sometimes offered cold on hot days, is served with a choice selection of cakes, breads, sweets and savouries.

Of course, I love to display all my tea paraphernalia – that is part of the fun. There is, for example, the embroidered, white on white, organdy tea-cosy cover I bought off the nuns in New Delhi, to say nothing of the tea caddy and jam jar acquired on a lucky Saturday from London's Portobello Road or the blue and white China plate, perfect for holding hot scones, found at a flea market in Bombay.

AN ANGLO-INDIAN BRUNCH

INDIAN-STYLE SCRAMBLED EGGS WITH POTATOES AND
CAULIFLOWER
SPICY CHICKEN LIVERS
GRILLED TOMATOES FLAVOURED WITH THYME
TOAST
TEA AND COFFEE

I was shooting a film in England recently and a few of us lucky actors were housed in a castle. Since we generally had to be on location for make-up and costumes shortly after sunrise, my breakfast, which I had in my room, was bleak. It had to be. At that hour, I could not stomach much more than toast and tea. Usually it was just a cup of tea – the tea in one hand, the film script in the other. The castle kitchen had, very sweetly, got me some good Darjeeling tea. That was all I wanted. My mind was totally on the scene I was to shoot that day.

But then I had a few days' break and my husband arrived from America. We slept late and came down to an enormous dining room to eat what my husband dearly wanted – a proper English breakfast. I had lost track of these breakfasts. Every single hotel in British India used to serve them (some still do). There would be porridge first, to be eaten with hot milk and sugar, then eggs, served with large English sausages, grilled liver, grilled kidneys, grilled tomatoes, and lots of toast, butter, marmalade and tea. We used to have these breakfasts in our own home in Delhi – and to this day, the taste of eggs – especially fried eggs – is inextricably linked in my mind to that of grilled tomatoes. If I remember correctly, our cook never *grilled* tomatoes. We did not have a grill. He just put them into a frying pan and scorched them a bit on both sides.

I have dispensed with the porridge here. If you want it, get a good quality Irish oatmeal, the slow-cooking kind. It takes about half an hour to cook. (A wonderful inn in England's Lake District cooks it slowly all night in a double boiler and then serves it the next morning with brown sugar and light cream.)

I have Indian-ized the British breakfast, something I (and a lot of other Indians) am quite prone to do. There is fresh ginger in the scrambled eggs, cumin in the chicken livers, and cayenne on the tomatoes.

This meal is very easy to put together, though you do have to do several things at the same time. If you have guests – or children – encourage them to wander into the kitchen to watch the toast and carry out the tea.

INDIAN-STYLE SCRAMBLED EGGS WITH POTATOES AND CAULIFLOWER
Serves 4–6

This is a Sunday favourite with our family. I cook the vegetables at my convenience in the morning and have them ready. Then, when we are all assembled in the dining room – usually for a rather late breakfast – I heat up the vegetables again, throw the beaten eggs into the pan, and quickly scramble them.

4 tablespoons/60ml vegetable oil
½ teaspoon/2.5ml whole cumin seeds
Half a medium-sized onion, peeled and finely chopped
1 medium-sized potato (about 4oz/115g), peeled and cut into ¼-in/6-mm dice
About 2 cups (6oz/180g) finely cut small florets of cauliflower (none longer than ¾in/2cm or wider than ½in/1.5cm)
½–1 fresh hot green chilli, finely chopped (optional)
1 teaspoon/5ml peeled and finely grated fresh ginger
Salt
Freshly ground black pepper
8 eggs, lightly beaten

Heat 3 tablespoons/45ml of the oil in a large non-stick frying pan over a medium flame. When hot, put in the cumin seeds. Let them sizzle for a few seconds. Put in the onion. Stir and fry until it softens slightly. Put in the potato. Stir and fry until the pieces are lightly browned. Now put in the cauliflower, green chilli and ginger. Stir and fry for 2 minutes. Add 2 tablespoons/30ml water and bring it to a simmer. Cover, turn the heat to low, and cook gently for about 10 minutes or until the cauliflower is just done, but still crisp and the potatoes are all cooked through. Stir several times during this period, replacing the cover each time. Uncover when done and turn the flame off. Dust lightly with salt and pepper. Stir to mix.

Just before eating, dust the beaten eggs with salt and black pepper to taste. Mix. Turn the flame under the vegetables to medium-high. Stir the vegetables around until they are heated through. Now, push them to the edges of the frying pan. Add the remaining tablespoon/15ml of oil and let it heat for a few seconds. Pour in the beaten eggs. Stir them around gently, scrambling them to the consistency you like. Mix in the vegetables during the last stages of the scrambling. Serve.

SPICY CHICKEN LIVERS
Serves 4–6

These livers may also be served on toast or buttered bread as a light snack or on on top of a small mound of slivered dressed cucumbers as a first course.

3 tablespoons/45ml olive oil
½ teaspoon/2.5ml whole cumin seeds
2 shallots, peeled and finely chopped
1 lb/450g chicken livers, trimmed and separated into 2 lobes each
½ teaspoon/2.5ml salt
Freshly ground black pepper
⅛ teaspoon cayenne pepper
¼ teaspoon finely crumbled dried sage
3 tablespoons/45ml plain yoghurt

Just before eating, heat the oil in a large frying pan on a high flame. When very hot, put in the cumin seeds. Five seconds later, put in the shallots. Stir once or twice. Now put in the chicken livers, spreading them out in a single layer in the pan. Sprinkle with half the salt and some black pepper, half the cayenne, and half the sage. Cook for about 1½–2 minutes. Turn them over and brown the second sides for 1½–2 minutes, sprinkling once again with the remaining salt, black pepper, cayenne and sage. The livers should brown on the outside and remain moist and slightly pink inside. Remove the livers to a bowl with a slotted spoon. Quickly add the yoghurt to the frying pan, turning down the heat a bit as you do so. Scrape up all the pan juices, stirring and mixing the yoghurt into them as you do so. Pour this sauce over the livers and toss them in the bowl.

GRILLED TOMATOES FLAVOURED WITH THYME
Serves 4–6

You can grill as many tomatoes as you think you might eat. If they are of a good size, I allow half per person. If they are smallish, I grill two halves per person. If they are red, ripe and of good flavour, just follow the recipe below. If they are of medium-quality, squeeze a little lemon juice (about 1 teaspoon/5ml for a good-sized tomato half) and sprinkle a pinch of sugar over them first, and then proceed.

Tomatoes (see note above)
Salt
Freshly ground black pepper
Cayenne pepper
½ teaspoon/2.5ml dried thyme
About ½ teaspoon/2.5ml any vegetable oil per half tomato

Preheat the grill (broiler).

Cut the tomatoes in half crosswise and set them out in a grilling (broiling) tray, cut side up. Sprinkle generously with salt, black pepper and cayenne pepper. Now sprinkle the thyme evenly over the top and dribble the oil over that. Place under the grill (broiler) and cook for 5–8 minutes or until browned on the top.

AT HOME ON SUNDAY WITH FRIENDS: A TEX-MEX BRUNCH

MARGARITAS OR FROSTY FRESH TOMATO JUICE
HUEVOS RANCHEROS (EGGS WITH SPICY TOMATO SAUCE)
STIR-FRIED NEW POTATOES
COFFEE AND TEA

This brunch has Tex-Mex overtones, complemented with a few, well-chosen Indian highlights. As guests come in, I offer them icy-cold margaritas in salt-rimmed glasses. It is a nice way to say 'Good morning'. The combination of salt and lime nudges one to awaken fully while the tequila – the clear and very potent tequila – keeps one mellow. For those who do not drink liquor – and many of my friends do not – I offer tomato juice (always fresh in the summer), lightly seasoned with ground roasted cumin seeds, the way I had it at mid-morning every single day during my childhood, or else freshly squeezed orange juice.

As guests poke at the Sunday paper, or mill around, I get the meal together. The spicy tomato sauce – *salsa*, as it is called in Mexico and Texas – is ready. I make it the night before. I also boil the potatoes the night before, cool, peel and dice them, then I bag them and put them in the refrigerator. The trick to having 'fresh coffee' at all hours I have learned from the brilliant and beautiful food consultant and cookbook author, Marion Cunningham. I simply make two batches (one decaffeinated), in the morning and store them in separate thermos flasks. The coffee stays hot and does not have that awful, reheated, I've-been-sitting-on-the-heat-too-long taste. All I have to do then is stir-fry the potatoes and when they are done, fry the eggs.

MARGARITAS

Serves 1–6

Margaritas are among my favourite drinks. They are made – for those of you who are unfamiliar with them – of Mexican tequila, and even though they go down as easily as a cold lemonade on a hot summer's day, they can pack a punch. Margaritas may be had 'straight up', 'on the rocks', or 'frozen'. In their 'frozen' state, they may, with a little less ice, be made thin enough to just flow – so they can be drunk – or they can be made as firm as a sorbet, firm enough to require a spoon. I sometimes serve them in the sorbet form at the end of a meal.

It is traditional to serve margaritas in salt-rimmed wine glasses. To do this, spread coarse salt on a plate. Rub the rim of a rounded wine glass with a cut lime in order to wet it and then turn it upside down in the salt to cover the rim completely. Set aside until you are ready to make the drink. First, the classic margarita, which combines tequila with Triple Sec, an orange-based sweet liqueur. I have here the recipes for one serving and for six servings (so you won't have to bother with too much calculation).

For One Serving

3 tablespoons/45ml (1 jigger or shot) tequila
1 tablespoon/15ml Triple Sec or Cointreau
1 tablespoon/15ml lime juice (you will need a bit more – or a cut lime – for wetting the rim)
¼ teaspoon extra-fine sugar (optional)

For Six Servings

½ pint/275ml tequila
3fl oz/75ml Triple Sec or Cointreau
3fl oz/75ml lime juice (you will need a bit more – or a cut lime – for wetting the rims)
4½ teaspoons/7.5ml extra-fine sugar (optional)

Put the tequila, Triple Sec, lime juice, sugar (if required) and ice (4–7 cubes for a single drink – a few handfuls for 6 drinks) into a cocktail shaker or electric blender. Shake or blend for a few seconds or until frothy and very cold. Strain and serve in pre-prepared glasses. This is a 'straight-up' margarita. To make an 'on-the-rocks', add a few ice cubes to each glass. To make 'frozen' margaritas, put all the ingredients plus about 4–7 ice cubes for a single drink, 3 teacups ice cubes for 6 drinks into a blender and blend until the ice cubes have turned to mush. Pour or spoon into prepared wine glasses and serve.

Here is a recipe for a not-so-classic margarita. This is how our neighbour the potter, Ron Dier, makes it, and uncommonly good and easy it is too. This recipe makes frozen or semi-frozen margaritas and serves 4 to 6 depending on the size of the portions. It does require access to frozen Minute-Maid limeade concentrate.

6fl oz/177ml tequila
6fl oz/177ml container of frozen limeade concentrate

Combine the tequila, frozen limeade and about three good-sized teacups of ice cubes in a blender. Blend until mushy. Serve in pre-prepared salt-rimmed wine glasses.

FROSTY FRESH TOMATO JUICE

Serves 6

There is nothing quite like thick, fresh tomato juice. It is so easy to make at home, specially during the height of the tomato season. Pick only red-ripe tomatoes. Slightly overripe tomatoes are perfect for juicing. If you have a juicing machine, you may use that, or else use my blender method.

2 lb/900g red, very ripe tomatoes, coarsely cubed
1½ tablespoons/22ml lime juice
¾ teaspoon/4ml salt – or to taste
Freshly ground black pepper
¾ teaspoon/4ml ground roasted cumin seeds (see page 189)
20–22 ice cubes

Put the tomatoes, lime juice, salt, pepper and cumin seeds into the container of an electric blender (you may have to do this in two batches). Blend until smooth. Empty into a large bowl. The juice will be very thick. Add the ice cubes. Stir and mix. Leave the ice cubes to melt until the juice has thinned out somewhat. I usually let the cubes melt completely. Taste for seasoning. Refrigerate until needed.

HUEVOS RANCHEROS (EGGS WITH SPICY TOMATO SAUCE)

Serves 6 or more

How can I ever forget the first time I had this dish? I was returning from Mexico where I had gone for the dual purpose of doing a film in Cuernavaca and acquiring a speedy divorce in Ciudad Juarez. The film (excellent, but alas unsung) required me to be the angel Lucifer – a beautiful woman in God's heaven and a contorted half-man, half-woman once banished to Hell. As I was in Hell for the greater portion of the film – or heading there – I found myself for almost six weeks suspended from rocky precipices with the aid of insecure harnesses, creeping on all fours over sharp lavic rocks and leaping with supposed abandon across overwhelming bodies of fire and water, all the time wearing 3-inch long nails and a beard across half my chin. (Yes, I have pictures.)

By the time I reached Juarez, I had bruises and cuts all over my body and half my face was red and sore from the wear and tear of daily beard removals. The other divorce-seekers – and there were thirty of us – looked no better. One girl, with a defiant ribbon in her hair, had a black eye, and a young man – he said he was a school teacher from New York – had a gash on his lip. I remember he wore striped socks that just wouldn't stay up. We were a pathetic lot. We all seemed to be on a conveyor belt with the one at the end disappearing every ten minutes behind a large wooden door. There wasn't much behind that door, just a small man at a big desk who shoved a lot of papers at me to sign without once giving me the benefit of a direct or indirect look.

Once that business was taken care of, I was taken across the border by car (all this had been arranged meticulously by a New York lawyer I had never met) and deposited in El Paso. My first positive act as a freshly divorced woman was to enter a coffee shop and order a late breakfast – Huevos Rancheros: two beautifully fried 'sunny-side-up' eggs, bathed in a hot, tangy, delicious sauce of chopped tomatoes, green chillies and fresh green coriander.

Fried eggs
I'm sure I do not have to tell you how to fry eggs. Suffice it to say that in our family we make them two ways. Our children, influenced by the Indian cooks of their childhood who cooked everything on a very high flame, like theirs crisp on the bottom with the whites quite firm and the yokes thick and creamy. My husband and I, on the other hand, do not like crisp-bottomed fried eggs. We do, however, also like firm whites and creamy yolks.

To make the more classic fried eggs, the kind my husband and I prefer, just cover the bottom of a non-stick frying pan lightly with oil and set it over medium heat. When hot, break in the eggs, as many as the pan will hold easily. Cook slowly until the whites are firm and the yolks are creamy. If an uncooked film persists on the top of the eggs, cover the pan for about five seconds. Lift the eggs out with a slotted spatula and serve.

To cook the crisp-bottomed fried eggs, cover the bottom of a non-stick frying pan with about ¹⁄₁₆in/2mm oil and set it to heat on a medium-high flame. When hot, break in as many eggs as the pan will hold easily. These eggs cook faster, especially their undersides. In order to cook the tops, tilt the pan frequently and, using a spoon, baste the tops of the eggs with hot oil. Lift the eggs out of the oil with a slotted spatula and serve.

Spicy sauce of uncooked tomatoes
I serve the sauce on the side so everyone can take the amount they want.

A 28oz/800g can peeled tomatoes
½ teaspoon/2.5ml salt or to taste
2–6 fresh hot green chillies, finely chopped
2 tablespoons/30ml finely chopped fresh green coriander (Chinese parsley)
Freshly ground black pepper

Lift the tomatoes out of the liquid in the can and chop them coarsely. (The juice from the can may be saved for a soup.) Put them in a bowl. Add all the other ingredients and mix well. Set aside (30 minutes to 12 hours) for the flavours to blend. Serve with the eggs.

STIR-FRIED NEW POTATOES
Serves 6

3½lb/1.5kg new or red potatoes, well scrubbed
4 tablespoons/60ml vegetable oil (peanut, groundnut, corn or olive)
2 teaspoons/10ml whole cumin seeds
2 tablespoons/30ml whole sesame seeds
1½ teaspoons/7.5ml salt
Freshly ground black pepper

Boil the potatoes in their jackets until just done. Drain and allow to cool. Without peeling, cut into good ½-in/1.5-cm cubes.

Heat the oil in a large wok or frying pan over a medium-high flame. When hot, put in the cumin seeds. Stir once and put in the sesame seeds. As soon as the sesame seeds begin to pop (this takes just a few seconds), put in the potatoes and salt. Stir and fry until the potatoes are lightly browned on all sides. Sprinkle black pepper over the top and toss again.

The trick with tea
Unlike the coffee, the tea I do make fresh and put in a tea-cosied teapot.

Talking of tea-cosied teapots, I have two teapots in the country, one a heavy ceramic one and the other an English bone china one. I had noticed that the tea from the teapots never tasted the same. The bone china pot always made better tea. I put this down to my own error in never getting the proportion of tea to water quite right in the ceramic pot.

One recent afternoon, Chhun Kern, a visiting friend, remarked on how good the tea was and I muttered something about how I get my tea fresh from India every month. She went on to ask if the teapot was bone china. Yes, it was, I answered. 'Well, that's it, then,' she said, looking like a wise lady from the Himalayas (which she is). It seems that a Pakistani friend of *hers* had told *her* that tea tastes best when made in a bone china teapot and the quality of my tea had just confirmed it!

We gather our information where we may. And this unscientific bit may be taken or left. I do, however, seriously recommend tea cosies if you drink tea.

I offer tea and coffee with the meal and then, once we have eaten the eggs, I offer it again with some cookies.

Overleaf
CLOCKWISE FROM THE TOP: MARGARITAS, STIR-FRIED NEW POTATOES, FROSTY FRESH TOMATO JUICE, HUEVOS RANCHEROS OR EGGS WITH SPICY TOMATO SAUCE

THE BEST OF NEW YORK CITY: A JEWISH BRUNCH

WONDERFUL BLOODY MARYS

EGGS SCRAMBLED IN A DOUBLE BOILER

KIPPERS SERVED ON A BED OF GLAZED ONIONS

BAGELS

CREAM CHEESE WITH SPRING ONIONS
(SCALLIONS) OR CHIVES

SMOKED SALMON

SLICED TOMATOES

COFFEE AND TEA

So you buy a few things and you make a few things. The bagels you buy, the best and freshest available. (Use frozen ones in a pinch, or use good-quality fresh bread instead.)

On top of the bagels (split in half, laterally) goes cream cheese, thickly laid, preferably with chives or spring onions (scallions) in it. On top of *that* goes the smoked salmon. Then you bite into it. How good it is!

When I first came to New York City almost three decades ago, Joanna (Mrs Dretzin) and I were struggling actresses. She was struggling a little less than I was, having already appeared with Charlton Heston in *The Ten Commandments*. I had appeared with nobody, was still off-Broadway, earning a pitiful $10 a week or some such worthy sum sacrificing myself eight times a week for my Art (with a capital A).

It was Joanna's father-in-law who cooked me my first 'Jewish' brunch. I was grateful for anything at the time, but *this* was, for me, the most delicious, exotic feast I had ever tasted. We started with Bloody Marys and then the rest of the meal descended like a deluge of wonders – bagels, cream cheese, salmon, red-ripe tomatoes, soft-soft scrambled eggs, and glory of glories, kippers served over a bed of soft, brown, almost caramelized onions.

Since the death of his father, Joanna's husband, Duff, has taken over the chef's Sunday *toque blanche* and so it is from him that I've elicited the finer points of this menu. Unable to resist, I've added a few minor touches of my own as well.

WONDERFUL BLOODY MARYS
Makes about 12 drinks

A Bloody Mary is a perky drink just perfect for brunches, lunches and hot summer dinners. For every serving, you will need a jigger (3 tablespoons/45ml) of vodka and half a cup of my specially seasoned tomato juice. Use a large wine glass or a highball glass for serving the cocktail.

For the Seasoned Juice

2¼ pints/1.25 litres canned tomato juice
About 25 shakes from a bottle of Worcestershire Sauce
About 10 dashes of Tabasco Sauce
4 teaspoons/20ml prepared horseradish
3–4 tablespoons/45–60ml lemon or lime juice
1½ teaspoons/7.5ml roasted and ground cumin seeds (see page 189)
Celery salt
Freshly ground black pepper

You Also Need

3 tablespoons/45ml (1 jigger) vodka per serving
Ice: 5–6 cubes per serving
4–5-in/10–12-cm long celery sticks – one per serving

In a large jug, combine the tomato juice, Worcestershire Sauce, Tabasco Sauce, horseradish, lemon juice, cumin seeds, celery salt and black pepper to taste. Stir to mix and check seasonings. You may wish to add a bit more of this or that. The juice can be mixed ahead of time, covered and refrigerated. To make each drink, pour the vodka into a glass, then pour in about 4fl oz/119ml/½ cup of the juice and add 5 or 6 ice cubes. Mix well. Stick in a piece of celery as a swizzle stick.

EGGS SCRAMBLED IN A DOUBLE BOILER
Serves 6

The eggs stay very moist when cooked this way.

10 large eggs
4 tablespoons/60ml milk
A few dashes of Worcestershire Sauce
A few dashes of Tabasco Sauce
Salt
Freshly ground black pepper
2oz/60g/¼ cup butter

Put the water in the bottom container of a double boiler and set to boil.

Put the eggs in a large bowl and beat lightly. Add the milk, Worcestershire Sauce, Tabasco Sauce, salt to taste and freshly ground black pepper.

Put the butter in the top section of the double boiler and set it over the bottom container. Let the butter melt and heat. Now put in the eggs. Stir very gently until thick, soft curds form. Serve immediately.

KIPPERS SERVED ON A BED of GLAZED ONIONS
Serves 6 as part of this brunch

Kippers – British smoked herrings – are delicious in all forms, but I like them best this way, sitting on a bed of browned, almost caramelized, onions. Sometimes I brown the onions just by themselves, the way I first had them 20 years ago in the Dretzin household, and at other times I add thinly sliced hot green chillies to give the dish some extra pep.

Alternatives to kippers included canned sardines (drained of oil) slices of smoked whitefish (available in Jewish delicatessens), and smoked eels. If the meal does not need to be kosher, you may even used smoked oysters or mussels, the kinds found in bottles and cans.

2 kippers weighing about 8oz/225g each
3oz/90g/⅓ cup butter
2 lb/900g onions, peeled and cut into very fine half-rings

1 fresh hot green chilli, cut into very thin
rounds (optional)

½ teaspoon/2.5ml salt

Freshly ground black pepper

½ teaspoon/2.5ml ground roasted cumin seeds
(see page 189)

Fillet the kippers: open one kipper up and cut the head off. Cut lengthwise into 2 halves. Most of the skeletal structure will be along one half. Start feeling you way under it with your fingers first and then with a knife. Cut it all away. Pull out the larger, loose bones on the second half of the fish, using a pair of tweezers if necessary. Do the same with the second kipper. Cut each half, crosswise, into 3 segments. Set aside.

Heat the butter over a medium-high flame in a large non-stick frying pan. Put in all the onions and the green chilli. Stir and fry until the onions just start to brown. Turn the heat to medium. Keep stirring and cooking until the onions have a lovely brown, glazed, almost caramelized appearance. Add the salt and some black pepper. Mix and turn off the flame.

Just before you eat, heat up the onions again. Lay the kipper slices over them in a single layer. Dust the kippers lightly with ground cumin and black pepper. Cover and heat the kippers through over a low flame. You do not need to cook them.

BAGELS
Serves 6

Allow 2 bagels per person. You may have some left over but they can easily be frozen. I like to buy plain bagels. Just make sure they are the freshest and best you can get. Slice each in half, laterally. If you cannot find bagels, use any good quality bread cut in slices.

CREAM CHEESE WITH SPRING ONIONS (SCALLIONS) OR CHIVES
Serves 6

This is always good to have around and maybe eaten on bagels or toast.

8oz/225g/1 cup plain cream cheese

2 tablespoons/30 ml very finely chopped spring
onions (scallions) or fresh chives

Mix the 2 ingredients together several hours or even a day ahead of time. Cover and refrigerate.

SMOKED SALMON
Serves 6

You should get at least 18 thin slices of smoked salmon, the best, least salty kind available. Arrange the slices prettily on a plate.

SLICED TOMATOES
Serves 6

Buy 3 large ripe tomatoes and then slice them fairly thinly. Arrange them in overlapping slices on a plate.

A SIMPLE TEA FROM MY STUDENT DAYS IN LONDON

SCONES WITH BUTTER (OR CLOTTED CREAM) AND JAM
DARJEELING TEA

To a teenager growing up in India, a scone seemed the most exotic of treats. It was so – well – foreign. Like tweeds, Wordsworth and the Royal Family, it was imbued with the aura of being quintessentially British. Even the way its name was pronounced – 'scon' – tickled me no end (I know now that it can be said two ways.)

I ate scones very rarely in India. The first time I had one was in a houseboat moored on the Jhelum River in the mountainous state of Kashmir. There were only two of us living on that houseboat, both of us good friends on holiday, both seventeen and both studying English Literature at a women's college in Delhi. If that sounds a bit daring for India in 1950, it wasn't really. Even though technically unchaperoned, we were guests of the state's Prime Minister. Houseboats in Kashmir function as small, private hotels so the owner/chef of our three-bedroom affair was more than anxious to please us. We were fed four times a day and at each meal we were asked what we'd like for the next. *That* made us feel very grown up. Many of the dishes offered were holdovers from colonial times when British families 'summered' in the 'hills'. The foods that excited *us* the most were, quite naturally, the ones that were the farthest from our daily diet in the Plains. When the cook mentioned 'rhubarb' or 'asparagus', he sent us into a tizzy of excitement. And the day he asked us if we would like scones for tea, we were practically hysterical with joyful anticipation. We could just see all those Bennett girls from Pride and Prejudice buttering their scones. Now *we* would do the same!

I liked the idea of the scone before I had the thing itself but once I'd taken my first bite of that crumbly, buttery delight, I was hooked for life.

Even today, my favourite tea consists of nothing more than freshly made scones washed down with 'the cup that cheers'. I serve this almost every other weekend to friends and family who visit us in the country.

SCONES WITH BUTTER (OR CLOTTED CREAM) AND JAM

Serves 4–6

It is best to serve these soon after they come out of the oven. I usually keep all the dry ingredients mixed and ready and then work in the butter, eggs and cream just before I bake. You will need a little bit of extra butter to grease the baking sheet.

8½oz/240g/2 cups plain (all-purpose) flour
2 teaspoons/10ml baking powder
2 tablespoons/30ml caster (superfine) sugar
¼ teaspoon salt
2oz/60g/4 tablespoons unsalted butter cut into small pieces
2 large eggs, beaten lightly
4fl oz/119ml/½ cup single (heavy) cream

Also to have at the table to eat with the scones

A dish of unsalted butter
A dish of clotted cream
Jars of your favourite jams (such as strawberry, raspberry and cherry)

Preheat oven to 425°F/220°C/Gas Mark 7.

Lightly butter a baking sheet and set aside.

Sift the flour, baking powder, sugar and salt into a bowl. Add the pieces of butter. Using a pastry blender or your finger tips, cut or rub in the butter until the mixture resembles coarse breadcrumbs. Add the eggs and cream and stir lightly until just blended. Do not overmix. Turn out on to a floured surface and knead lightly for half a minute or so. Roll out or pat into a ¾in/2mm round. Using a 2–2½in/5–6mm biscuit cutter, press out small rounds. Lightly knead the trimmings, roll out again and cut as many more rounds as you can. Place on buttered baking sheet and bake in the top third of the oven for about 15 minutes.

DARJEELING TEA

Serves 6

There are many teas that I enjoy: A bowl of Japanese *matcha*, green powdered tea, whipped up to a froth, is exceedingly elegant; half fermented Chinese White Peony tea with its hint of bitterness is wonderfully bracing; and keemun tea, a Chinese black tea sometimes served with a dried rose floating in it is as aromatic as it is visually pleasing. However, it is the slightly smoky taste of highgrown, unblended Darjeeling tea that I find most satisfying.

Perhaps it is because I grew up with this tea that I turn to it so frequently. Sometimes I serve it somewhat weak and plain, and at other times quite strong with additions of milk and sugar. You could also have it with lemon and honey as many of my friends do.

When making the tea, boil some fresh water. Then rinse out the teapot with the boiling water to warm it up. For 6 good-sized cups of tea, put in 6–7 teaspoons/30–35ml of the tea leaves into the teapot. Add about 6 teacups of *boiling* water. Put the lid back on the teapot and then cover it with a tea-cosy. Let the tea brew for about 5 minutes before serving it.

A TEA FROM MY INDO-BRITISH CHILDHOOD

LEMON TARTS
SPICY CUCUMBER SANDWICHES
TEA

When we were children, our 'tea' consisted of a tall glass of hot milk in the winter and the same tall glass filled with cold milk in the summer. With it we usually had a slice of bread and butter or else some toast liberally spread with sweet jam or tart and spicy mango pickle! As a treat, specially if a guest was going to drop in, my mother sent the driver off to New Delhi (we lived in Old Delhi) to pick up some Indian sweets from Bengali Market and some 'pastries' from Davicos or Wengers, two well-established, Indo-British tea restaurants. (The former even had a ballroom with tea dances held on the weekends.) A cake-man who travelled with a tin trunk strapped to the back of his bicycle supplied the pound cake. Our own cook made the small, dainty cucumber or chicken sandwiches without which no 'proper' tea could be quite complete. Our sandwiches were spiced up and Indianized, but then the whole meal was an amazing blend of East and West that only colonial India could produce!

Of all the 'pastries', my favourites were the lemon tarts. Small – each the size of three small bites – they were filled with the most delicious tart and buttery lemon curd. It was the old-fashioned lemon curd, made mostly with egg yolks and butter. (I have used a nineteenth century recipe here.)

What follows is a very reduced version of my Indian tea. People eat much less nowadays and since I do all the preparation myself, I like to keep it manageable so it is fun for my guests – and for me! You may serve any tea of your choice with this meal.

LEMON TARTS

Serves 6

If you like, you could fill half the tarts with your favourite jam and the other half with lemon curd. Since the lemon curd can last for several weeks in the refrigerator, my recipe for it is rather generous. It makes enough to fill a 1½ pint/1 litre/4 cup jar. You can make it well in advance.

For the Filling

6 medium-sized lemons
6 eggs
1 pound/450g/2¼ cups castor (superfine) sugar
6oz/180g/12 tablespoons unsalted butter at room temperature

For the Pastry

8oz/225g/2 cups less 1 tablespoon plain (all-purpose) flour
2oz/50g/5 tablespoons castor (superfine) sugar
5oz/125g/10 tablespoons unsalted butter, slightly softened
1 egg

The filling

Grate the rind off 4 of the lemons and squeeze out the juice from all 6. Set both aside separately.

Put sufficient water in the bottom half of a double boiler and set it to heat. It should not overflow when the top half is placed over it.

Place the top half of the double boiler on the counter in front of you and put into it 2 whole eggs as well as the yolks of the remaining 4 eggs. (You do not need the other 4 whites.) Beat the eggs lightly with a whisk. Add the sugar and beat lightly to mix. Strain in the lemon juice. Add the grated rind and the butter. Put the top of the double boiler over the bottom half. Now move the whisk around in one direction until the mixture turns thick and gluelike. This can take 20–30 minutes. Lift off the top of double boiler and let it cool off just slightly. Now pour the curd into a clean jar. Set the jar in a bowl of cold water. Stir the curd gently as it cools. The jar can now be closed and refrigerated. The curd should keep 2–3 weeks.

The pastry

Sift the flour and sugar into a large bowl. Cut the butter into small pieces and add it to the bowl. Using a pastry blender or your finger tips, cut or rub in the butter until the mixture resembles coarse breadcrumbs. Beat the egg and stir it into the mixture with a fork. Flour hands and gather the mixture together into a ball. Knead lightly with the heel of the palm. Form a ball and then flatten it a bit. Cover with waxed paper and refrigerate for 30 minutes or longer.

Lightly butter 18 tart moulds, each mould about 2½–2¾in/6½–7¼cm in diameter and fairly shallow. (I have trays with 12 moulds each.) Lay a sheet of waxed paper about 1ft/30cm long on your work surface. Put the dough on it. Cover it with another sheet of waxed paper of the same length. Roll out the dough between the sheets of paper. Roll from the centre out, loosening both papers several times and turning the dough over 2–3 times, until you have a round that is somewhere between ⅛ and ¼in/3mm–5mm thick. Remove the top sheet of paper and, using a pastry cutter, cut circles that are about 2¾in/7¼cm in diameter and lay them in the tart moulds. Refrigerate moulds for 30 minutes.

Preheat oven to 400°F/200°C/Gas mark 6.

Remove moulds from the refrigerator. Fill each tart shell about ⅔ full with about 2 scant teaspoons/10ml of the lemon curd. Bake on the middle shelf of the oven for 15 minutes. Let the tarts cool a bit before you ease them out of their moulds.

SPICY CUCUMBER SANDWICHES
Serves 6

It is best to make these with fine textured white sandwich bread though fine textured brown bread would do as well. If you are in the habit of baking your own bread, you can easily convert it into the more squared off sandwich loaf this way: Let your dough rise in the usual way the first time. Then, for the second rising, put it into as rectangular a tin as you can find, one without sloping sides. Cover this tin, first with a sheet of oiled foil (oiled side down) and then with a baking sheet. Put an oven-proof weight on the baking sheet. Bake with the cover and weight still on top of the bread tin.

About 8in/20cm cucumber or 2–3 pickling cucumbers, depending upon their size
Salt
3oz/90g/6 tablespoons unsalted butter, softened
½ teaspoon/2.5ml Dijon-style mustard
1 tablespoon/15ml lemon juice
1 fresh, hot green chili (or more), very finely minced or ¼ teaspoon cayenne pepper
2 tablespoons/30ml very finely minced fresh green coriander (Chinese parsley) plus a few extra sprigs for garnishing
Freshly ground black or white pepper to taste
12 slices of soft, fine textured white or wholewheat bread, each about ²⁄₁₀in/½cm thick thick

Peel the cucumber and cut it into paper-thin slices. (I use the slicing blade of a food processor or a mandoline.) Put the slices into a wide, shallow bowl or into a soup plate. Add ½ teaspoon/2.5ml salt and toss. Put a small plate on top of the cucumbers and place a weight on top of the plate. Set aside for 1 hour. Drain the cucumber slices and pat them dry.

While the cucumbers are salting, get your spiced butter ready. In a bowl, mix the butter, mustard, lemon juice, green chili and green coriander (Chinese parsley). Add salt and pepper to taste. Mix again.

Butter the bread slices with this mixture. Lay the cucumber slices in slightly overlapping rows on 6 slices of bread and then invert the other 6 over them to make sandwiches. Cut off all the crusts and then cut each sandwich into 4 triangles or 4 squares. Arrange in a plate and garnish with the green sprigs.

A TEA WITHOUT TEA

LASSI, A YOGHURT DRINK
SAVOURY COOKIES

A typist came to work for me one day who refused all offers of tea and coffee. It turned out that she did not drink anything with caffein in it. The typist was American but she made me think back to my childhood in India where I knew many such people. My mother for one never touched tea. What did she drink then? She had cold milk flavoured with almonds and cardamom, ginger tea with honey, fresh limeade and lassi, a nourishing, cooling, drink made with diluted yoghurt which takes as long to make as it takes to turn on the blender or stir with a whisk.

Lassi can be served both sweet and salty. I prefer the salty one. My typist loved the sweet one. I serve both very simply with some savoury Indian cookies.

LASSI, A YOGHURT DRINK
Serves 4

You can use both whole milk yoghurt and low fat yoghurt to make this drink.

The Basic Lassi

8fl oz/237ml/1 cup plain yoghurt
1¼ pint/720ml/3 cups ice-cold water

Put the yoghurt and water into the container of a blender and blend until smooth. If you do not have a blender, put the yoghurt in a bowl. Add the water very slowly as you beat with a whisk or a fork.

Salty Lassi

To the basic lassi, add about 1 teaspoon/5ml ground, roasted cumin seeds (see page 189), about ½ teaspoon/2.5ml salt and some freshly ground black pepper. Stir to mix or blend.

Sweet Lassi

To the basic lassi, add about 3 tablespoons/45ml sugar (or to taste) and a few drops of rose essence or 1 teaspoon/5ml orange blossom water. If you cannot find these flower flavourings use a few drops of any other essence that you like. Stir to mix or blend.

SAVOURY COOKIES
Makes about 28

In India these cookies are deep-fried. I often prepare the dough with all the Indian ingredients, but instead of deep-frying, I bake them.

Here is my revised recipe:

7oz/200g/1¾ cup plain (all-purpose) flour
¾ teaspoon/3.75ml salt
1 tablespoon/15ml coarsely crushed black peppercorns
¼ teaspoon dried thyme
¼ pound/110g/8 tablespoons ice-cold unsalted butter cut into small pieces
2fl oz/59ml/¼ cup ice-cold water

Sift the flour and salt into a bowl. Scatter in the crushed peppercorns, thyme and pieces of butter. Using a pastry blender or the tips of your fingers, cut or rub in the butter until the mixture resembles coarse breadcrumbs. Slowly add the water as you gather the dough into a loose ball. Lift the ball out with floured hands and place on a floured work surface. Knead quickly with the heel of your hand for a minute and then gather the dough into a ball. Flatten the ball somewhat. Wrap it in waxed paper and refrigerate it for about half an hour.

Preheat oven to 425°F/220°C/Gas Mark 7.

Flour your work surface again and roll out the dough until you have a ¼in/½cm thick round. Use a pastry cutter that is 2½in/6cm in diameter and cut out as many cookies as you can. Gather up the trimmings, roll out again and cut out more cookies. Put the cookies on a baking sheet or sheets and prod them all with a fork. (You may have to do this in two batches. Keep cookies you are not working on in the refrigerator.)

Put cookie sheet or sheets in the oven and bake for about 20 minutes or until golden and crisp. Cool and store in an airtight tin.

DESSERTS AND FRUIT

Desserts can be quite simple. Fresh, home-made cookies served with nicely brewed cups of coffee or seasonal berries served with honey and icecream can be just as satisfying as an elaborate moussecake.

I let the time and energy at my disposal determine what my dessert should be. If I am very rushed, I serve no dessert at all, just fruit, such as slices of the best pineapple or mangoes that I can find. Sometimes, when the meal warrants it, I serve fruit with cheese. A beautifully formed, juicy pear served with a wedge of ripe, unpasteurised Brie from Normandy or red and green bunches of grapes served with squares of Italian Taleggio or a fully ripe peach offered with the creamlike mascarpone, also from Italy, are not only beautiful to behold but utterly delicious.

With careful planning, even the more complicated desserts can be made without pain. Tarts for example. I bake extra empty shells whenever I have a little time and then I freeze them. They keep very well. Whenever a tart is called for, I pull a shell out of the freezer, pop it into the oven to crisp it up and then fill it with strawberries or raspberries. Nothing else is needed other than a quick application of red-currant glaze over the top. And perhaps some whipped cream.

COOL YOGHURT CREAM WITH FRUIT
Serves 6–8

This dessert comes from my neighbour, Roberta Gardner. I have added a little bit of ground cardamom to make it more aromatic and to give it a slight taste of India. To grind cardamom seeds, take 6 to 8 pods of cardamom and peel them. Then, either pulverize the seeds in a mortar or else put them between two sheets of waxed paper and crush them with the wide side of a hammer.

Since this is a jellied dessert, you should set it in a serving dish. I like to use a large, relatively shallow bowl, so the wide open surface of the dessert can be decorated with plenty of fruit. The dish I use has a 2-pt/1.14-litre/5-cup capacity.

As far as the fruit is concerned, I have a weakness for sliced, sweet oranges, but a combination of strawberries and oranges or oranges and bananas, or crushed, sweetened rasperries or sliced, ripe mangoes may also be used.

¾pt/425ml/2 cups plain yoghurt
¾pt/425ml/2 cups half and half mixture of single (heavy) cream and milk ('Half And Half' in USA)
7oz/200g/1 cup sugar
¼ teaspoon ground cardamom seeds (see note above)
1 tablespoon/15ml gelatine powder
2 large, sweet oranges
6–8 strawberries (optional)

Put the yoghurt in a bowl and beat lightly with a fork until smooth and creamy.

Combine the cream-milk mixture (or 'Half And Half'), sugar and ground cardamom in a pot and heat over a medium flame until the sugar has dissolved and the mixture is nicely warm to the touch. Take off the cooker (stove).

Meanwhile, dissolve the gelatine in 4 tablespoons/60ml cold water and add that to the cream and milk mixture. Stir to mix. Beat in the yoghurt. Pour into a wide, shallow serving dish with a 2-pt/1.14-litre/5-cup capacity. Cover and chill for several hours until set.

Just before serving, peel the oranges with a knife so that all the white pith is removed and then cut them crosswise into thin slices. Cut each slice into half.

Slice the strawberries if you are using them.

Ring the bowl with overlapping slices of oranges and strawberries. You may also put some fruit in the centre of the dish.

MELON AND GINGER SORBET
Serves 6–8

A distinctive and delicious combination of flavours. This recipe is best made with gallia melons. If these are not available, a large ripe honeydew would do.

8oz/225g/1⅓ cups castor sugar
3oz/75g fresh ginger, sliced thinly
2 tablespoons/30ml lemon juice
2 medium-sized gallia melons
2 egg whites

Put 2pt/1 litre/4 cups water and the sugar in a large pan. Heat gently to dissolve the sugar, making sure there are no granules on the side of the pan. When all the sugar has dissolved, bring to a boil and boil for 5 minutes. Remove the pan from the heat. Add the ginger slices and lemon juice to the syrup and allow to cool. Strain.

Remove the pips from the melon, scoop out the flesh, and liquidize or process the fruit until smooth.

Mix the fruit purée and sugar syrup together. Put into a plastic container suitable for the freezer and freeze until slushy – about 2–3 hours, depending how cold the freezer is. Stir occasionally at this stage.

Beat the egg whites until fairly stiff. Fold carefully into the fruit mixture. Freeze again, stirring 2–3 times as this helps to give a better texture.

Leave to become quite frozen.

Remove from the freezer and put in the refrigerator for 30–40 minutes before serving.

DEVIL'S FOOD CAKE
Serves 8–10

This moist cake is a special treat.

6oz/175g/1½ cup plain (all-purpose) flour
2oz/50g/½ cup cocoa
½ teaspoon/2.5ml bicarbonate of soda
6oz/175ml/¾ cup soft margarine
6oz/175g/1¼ cup dark soft brown sugar
4fl oz/120ml/½ cup golden syrup
2 eggs, well beaten
2oz/50g/¾ cup ground almonds
6fl oz/150ml/¾ cup milk

Frosting

6oz/175g/1½ cup icing (confectioners') sugar, sifted
1 egg white
1 tablespoon/15ml golden syrup
4 teaspoons/20ml lemon juice
2 tablespoons/30ml orange juice
Pinch of salt

Line the base and sides of an 8in/20cm diameter, 2.5in/7cm height springform cake tin with greaseproof paper.

Preheat oven to 300°F/150°C/Gas Mark 2.

Sift the flour, cocoa and bicarbonate of soda into a bowl. In another bowl cream the margarine and sugar until light and fluffy. Beat in golden syrup then gradually add the eggs and a little of the sifted flour. Beat in remaining cake ingredients and pour into prepared cake tin.

Bake on the centre shelf of the preheated oven for 1 hour 35–45 minutes or until a fine skewer inserted in the centre comes out clean.

Turn out on to a wire rack to cool, and gently remove the paper.

The frosting

Combine the icing sugar, egg white, syrup, lemon juice, orange juice and salt in a heatproof bowl. Whisk over boiling water for 5 minutes, or until the frosting stands in peaks. Remove the bowl from the pan and whisk the frosting until cool.

Swirl the frosting over the cold cake.

If liked, decorate with grated chocolate or chocolate curls.

STRAWBERRY AND RHUBARB TART
Serves 4

Are we not lucky that these two perfectly matched fruits come into season at about the same time!

Bake the pastry case blind, using old beans specially kept for this purpose.

Pastry

8oz/225g/2 cups plain (all-purpose) flour plus more for dusting
5oz/125g/½ cup plus 2 tablespoons butter, slightly softened
2oz/50g/5 tablespoons castor (superfine) sugar
1 medium egg
Baking beans

Filling

12oz/350g fresh rhubarb, trimmed weight
2oz/50g/5 tablespoons castor sugar
2 strips orange peel
2 teaspoons/10ml arrowroot (cornstarch)
8fl oz/237ml/1 cup redcurrant jelly
1¼lb/675g fresh strawberries, washed and hulled

Sift the flour and sugar into a large bowl. With your finger tips or a pastry blender, rub in the butter until the mixture resembles fine breadcrumbs. Beat the egg and stir it into the mixture with a fork. Flour the hands and gather the mixture into a ball. Knead lightly on a floured surface with the heel of the palm. Form a ball. Cover with greaseproof/waxed paper and refrigerate for 30 minutes.

Preheat oven to 400°F/200°C/Gas Mark 6.

Lightly flour a surface. Roll the pastry out just large enough to line the base and sides of a 9-in/23-cm loose-bottomed fluted tart tin. Lightly prick the base. Carefully lay a piece of foil or greaseproof paper inside the pastry case making sure it comes up the sides and fill with the baking beans.

Bake just above the centre of the preheated oven for 15 minutes. Remove the foil or paper and beans and cook for a further 10 minutes to dry out the pastry. Allow to cool.

Meanwhile, trim and wash the rhubarb, and cut into 1-in/2-cm lengths. Place in a saucepan with the sugar, orange peel and 4 tablespoons/60ml water. Cover and cook gently for about 5–

8 minutes until the rhubarb is just tender. Remove the rhubarb to a plate with a slotted spoon, letting the juices drain back into the pan. Remove the orange peel.

In a small bowl blend the arrowroot with 1 tablespoon/15ml cold water. Add a little of the rhubarb juice, and mix it in. Now pour this mixture into the pan with most of the rhubarb juice. Bring slowly to the boil, stirring, and cook until thickened and clear. Remove pan from the heat, cool slightly and return the rhubarb to the thickened juice.

Gently melt the redcurrant jelly and brush a little over the base and sides of the pastry. Remove the flan case from the tin and place on a serving plate.

Spread the rhubarb on the base, arrange the prepared strawberries over the top and brush with the remaining melted jelly, heating again if necessary.

This is best eaten while the pastry is still crisp.

FRESH ORANGE SLICES WITH A GINGERY YOGHURT SAUCE
Serves 4

There is nothing quite like a good, juicy orange and it makes a perfect dessert if you wish to eat lightly. Orange slices can be served with absolutely nothing on them or you may, as we often do in India, transform them into a salad-cum-dessert by sprinkling them with a little salt, pepper, roasted and ground cumin (I *always* have that handy) and serving them with a yoghurt sauce spiked with fresh ginger.

4 oranges, peeled and left whole
Salt
Freshly ground black or white pepper
Ground roasted cumin seeds (see page 189)
Cayenne pepper
8fl oz/237ml/1 cup plain yoghurt
4 teaspoons/20ml sugar
1 teaspoon/5ml peeled and very finely grated fresh ginger

DESSERTS LEFT TO RIGHT: STRAWBERRY AND RHUBARB TART, DEVIL'S FOODCAKE

Cut the oranges crosswise into 5–6 slices each, depending on their size. Cut each slice in half crosswise. Sprinkle one side very lightly with salt, pepper, cumin and cayenne. Arrange slices in a slightly overlapping circle on four individual plates, leaving some empty space in the centre. Cover and refrigerate.

Put the yoghurt in a bowl and beat with a fork until smooth and creamy. Add the ginger, sugar and a light sprinkling of salt, pepper, cayenne and ground roasted cumin seeds. Stir to mix. Just before serving, put a generous dollop of this sauce in the centre of each plate of fruit.

LIME AND LEMON SORBET
Serves 4–6

There is nothing quite like a refreshing sorbet to end a meal. This recipe could be made with all limes or all lemons, but a combination of the two is best of all.

4 limes
2 lemons
8oz/225g/1¼ cups castor (superfine) sugar
1 egg white
A little green colouring (optional)

Finely grate the rind from the lemons and limes and squeeze out the juice. Strain this juice.

Put 1¼pt/750ml/3 cups water and the sugar in a fairly large pan. Heat gently to dissolve the sugar, making sure there are no granules on the side of the pan. When all the sugar has dissolved, bring to the boil and boil for 5 minutes. Remove pan from the heat. Stir in the grated rind and the lemon-lime juice. Cool. Add a few drops of green colouring if you so desire.

Pour this mixture into a plastic container suitable for the freezer and freeze until slushy. This can take maybe 2–3 hours, depending on how cold the freezer is. Stir occasionally.

Beat the egg white until fairly stiff. Fold it carefully into the fruit juice mixture and freeze.

It helps to give a better, less grainy texture, if you beat it 2 or 3 times during the final freezing stage, while it can still be stirred, then leave until really frozen.

Remove from the freezer and put in the refrigerator for about 30–40 minutes before serving.

If liked, decorate either with extra slices of lime or with frosted mint or lemon geranium leaves.

These are made by lightly brushing the leaves with egg white, dusting with caster sugar and allowing to dry. They need to be done well in advance, but are really worth the trouble as they look so effective.

CHOCOLATE AND WALNUT COOKIES
Makes about 30

These are quick to make and a great favourite with the family. I serve them frequently with coffee at the end of a meal in place of a dessert. They keep very well in an airtight tin.

4oz/100g/½ cup butter, softened
2oz/50g/½ cup light soft brown sugar
1 egg, well beaten
5oz/125g/1 cup plus 2 tablespoons self-raising flour
2oz/50g/½ cup walnuts, chopped
4oz/100g/¾ cup plain chocolate polka dots (chocolate chips)

Preheat oven to 350°F/180°C/Gas Mark 4.

Cream the butter and sugar until light and fluffy. Beat in the egg, then sift in the flour.

Mix in the walnuts and chocolate, using a fork to make it easier.

Place small teaspoonfuls fairly well apart on greased baking sheets, flatten slightly with a fork, and bake in the preheated oven for 12–15 minutes, until golden brown. It may be necessary to cook in two batches.

Transfer to a wire rack to cool.

PEARS POACHED IN A SAFFRON SYRUP
Serves 4–8

These pears, which I first made with the purest saffron from Kashmir, are heavenly. They turn a rich gold colour and are suffused with the heady aromas of both saffron and cardamom, amongst the most prized spices in the world.

7oz/100g/1 cup sugar
6 whole cardamom pods
¼ teaspoon good-quality saffron (the threads)
3 tablespoons/45ml lemon juice
4 firm pears

Combine the sugar, 15fl oz/425ml/2 cups water, cardamom pods, saffron and lemon juice and put in a shallow, but wide, pot. Bring to a simmer and cook gently until the sugar melts. Peel the pears, halve them and core them. As you cut them, put them into the simmering syrup. Cover and cook gently for 25 minutes. Every now and then, turn them gently or spoon syrup over them. Carefully take the pears out of the liquid and arrange them in a serving dish in a single layer, cut side down. Cook the syrup down until it is reduced to about 8fl oz/237ml/1 cup. Pour this over the pears. Cool.

ICE CREAM AND BERRIES WITH HONEY

In the summer, the countryside is bursting over with local berries – blackberries growing by cornfields, raspberries spreading their thin, prickly arms around ponds and blueberries growing under netted supervision, so that our feathered friends may not devour them.

Here is my favourite way of consuming these summer offerings: for each serving, I put a scoop or two of vanilla ice cream in a bowl. Then I throw in a handful of berries. On top of that, I dribble a good tablespoon or two of honey.

Our honey might come from our neighbour's the Gardners' house, but it actually belongs to both our families – or so we like to think. You see, they take the trouble to raise the bees and squeeze out the honey from dozens of honeycombs. But *we* take the trouble to raise the flowers from which the bees steal the honey in the first place. Throughout the sunny part of the year, there they are, buzz, buzz, buzz, stealing from our apple blossoms in the spring, stealing from our lavender in the summer, and stealing from our mallow right into the golden autumn. We do appreciate getting some of the honey back to spread upon our berries.

Overleaf
DESSERTS LEFT TO RIGHT: CHOCOLATE AND WALNUT COOKIES, LIME AND LEMON SORBET, FRESH ORANGE SLICES WITH A GINGERY YOGHURT SAUCE

THE BEST STRAWBERRY SHORTCAKE
Serves 12

The basic recipe for this comes from my father-in-law and how good it is too!

For the Strawberries

3½lb/1.5kg/about 4pt fresh strawberries
3 tablespoons/45ml lemon juice
½ teaspoon/2.5ml grated lemon rind
5oz/150g/¾ cup castor (superfine) sugar, plus another 3½oz/100g/½ cup for dipping whole strawberries

For the Shortcake

A little unsalted butter for greasing the baking tray
12½oz/350g/2½ cups plain (all-purpose) flour, plus more for dusting
2 tablespoons/30ml baking powder
2 tablespoons/30ml sugar
A pinch of salt
6oz/180g/¾ cup unsalted butter, cut into thin pats
2 large eggs, lightly beaten
¼pt/150ml/⅔ cup plain yoghurt, lightly beaten until smooth
1 teaspoon/5ml vanilla extract

You Also Need

¾pt/425ml/2 cups cream for whipping

Pick out 12 even-sized strawberries. Do not hull them. Wash and set aside in refrigerator. Hull and wash the remaining strawberries and then slice them. Put the sliced strawberries into a bowl. Add lemon juice, lemon rind, and 5oz/ 150g/¾ cups sugar. Toss. Cover and refrigerate.

Preheat the oven to 450°F/230°C/Gas Mark 8.

Lightly grease a biscuit (cookie) sheet or a baking tray with butter and set aside. Sift 10oz/ 280g/2 cups of the flour, the baking powder, sugar and salt into a bowl. Add the butter and with your fingertips or a pastry blender mix it in until the flour resembles coarse breadcrumbs. Make a well in the centre and pour in the beaten eggs, yoghurt and vanilla. Mix with a wooden spoon. Sift the remaining 2½oz/70g/½ cup flour over the mixture and fold it in with the spoon.

Empty the dough out on to a lightly floured surface. Dust a little more flour on top of it and then roll it out or push with the tips of your fingers until you have a round that is about ½– ¾in/1.5–2cm thick. Using a biscuit (cookie) cutter, cut 3-in/8-cm rounds. Place the rounds on the baking tray. Collect the remaining dough into a ball. Roll out again until ½–¾-in/ 1.5–2-cm thick, and cut out more rounds. Do this again until you have used up all the dough. You should have around 12–13 small 'cakes'. Place in the oven and bake for 15 minutes.

When you get ready to serve, whip the cream. Split each little cake in half as you would a scone or muffin and put the bottom halves on individual serving plates. Spoon a very generous portion of the cut strawberries and strawberry juice over them. Put some whipped cream over the strawberries. Now put the 'caps' or upper part of the cakes on top of the cream. Top this with a few more sliced strawberries and some more whipped cream. Put the 3½oz/100g/½ cup fine sugar in a small bowl. Take one whole strawberry at a time and dip it into the sugar. Place one such dipped strawberry on the very top of each little cake, hull-side down. Serve immediately.

Overleaf
THE BEST STRAWBERRY SHORTCAKE

To Roast Sesame Seeds

Put a small cast-iron frying pan to heat over a medium flame. Put in 1-4 tablespoons/15–60ml sesame seeds, according to the amount your recipe requires. Stir and cook until the seeds are lightly browned. They tend to fly around as they roast: you can put a loose cover over them.

To Roast And Grind Whole Cumin Seeds

Put a small cast-iron frying pan to heat over a medium flame. Put in 4 tablespoons/60ml or more of whole cumin seeds. Stir and cook them until they turn a few shades darker or until you smell a wonderful, roasted aroma. Empty the seeds into a dish and let them cool a bit. Now put them into the container of a spice grinder or clean coffee grinder and grind as finely as possible. Store in a clean jar with a tight-fitting lid. Use as needed. (Keep this handy in the kitchen at all times. It is wonderful.)

INDEX OF RECIPES